ASIAN AMERICAN
RACIAL REALITIES
IN BLACK AND WHITE

ASIAN AMERICAN RACIAL REALITIES IN BLACK AND WHITE

Bruce Calvin Hoskins

FIRST**FORUM**PRESS
A DIVISION OF LYNNE RIENNER PUBLISHERS, INC. • BOULDER & LONDON

Published in the United States of America in 2011 by
FirstForumPress
A division of Lynne Rienner Publishers, Inc.
1800 30th Street, Boulder, Colorado 80301
www.firstforumpress.com

and in the United Kingdom by
FirstForumPress
A division of Lynne Rienner Publishers, Inc.
3 Henrietta Street, Covent Garden, London WC2E 8LU

© 2011 by FirstForumPress. All rights reserved

Library of Congress Cataloging-in-Publication Data
Hoskins, Bruce Calvin.
  Asian American racial realities in black and white / Bruce Calvin Hoskins.
  Includes bibliographical references and index.
  ISBN 978-1-935049-39-5 (hardcover: alk. paper) 1. Asian
Americans—Social conditions. 2. Racially mixed people—United
States—Social conditions. 3. Asian Americans—Race identity. 4. Asian
Americans—Ethnic identity. 5. Racially mixed people—Race identity—United
States. 6. Racially mixed people—Ethnic identity—United States 7. United
States—Race relations. 8. United States—Ethnic relations. I. Title.
  E184.A75H67 2011
  305.895'073—dc23   2011018512

British Cataloguing in Publication Data
A Cataloguing in Publication record for this book
is available from the British Library.

This book was produced from digital files prepared by the author
using the FirstForumComposer.

Printed and bound in the United States of America

 The paper used in this publication meets the requirements
of the American National Standard for Permanence of
Paper for Printed Library Materials Z39.48-1992.

5 4 3 2 1

*To my Lord and savior Jesus Christ,
for with him all things are possible;*

*To my wife, Alice, the love of my life
and my constant support;*

*To my mother, Miyoko,
who raised three children by herself in a
foreign country;*

*And to my children, Michael, Riley, Carter, and Alana,
the four people for whom
I am trying to make the world a better place.*

Contents

1 Introduction 1
2 Internal Racial Identity 23
3 External Racial Identity 57
4 The External Context of Racial Identity Formation 79
5 Learning Racial Hierarchy 105
6 Conclusion 139

Appendixes
A: How the Sample Was Generated *143*
B: Interview Questions for Multiracial Persons *145*
C: Interview Questions for Interracially
  Married Parents *149*
Bibliography *151*
Index *160*

1
Introduction

I have seen myself as black all of my life; from the friends that I kept, to the sports that I played, to the music that I listened to and to the way that I spoke. I have never had a reason to doubt my blackness, until one day, while working in a math learning center at a community college, I helped an older Japanese woman with her math. As I assisted her, I noticed that she often made notes in *kanji* (Japanese handwriting) beside the instructions in her math book. When she saw that I observed this, she immediately apologized and told me that she wrote notes in the margins so that she could understand the directions. I tried to put her at ease by telling her it was not a problem and that my mother wrote notes like that all the time. After a moment of silence, she finally asked me the nationality of my mother. When I told her that my mother was Japanese, without hesitation she said, "Oh, that is why you are so good at math!"

This woman's surprise reveals a personal and social understanding that black people are not supposed to be good at math, while people of Japanese heritage are skilled at math. What it also demonstrated was that somewhere in her mind she questioned how a "black" man could be so good at math. My assumed race did not fit my known abilities, aptitudes, and attitudes. Simply stated, I did not make racial sense to her.

However, once my racial background was revealed, her common sense notions of race needed to form a new "racial logic" surrounding people of multiracial backgrounds: that people who are black and Japanese are good at math too. This understanding of race and racial hierarchy made me rethink my entire past regarding my assumption that I was black and that everyone treated me like I was black. Did my black friends think that I was good at school in general, but math specifically because I was Japanese? Did my white and Asian friends think the same thing? Did people actively wonder how a black man could be so good at math? How many people came to the same conclusion when they found out I was of black and Japanese heritage because I was too smart for a black person? Also, what would have been different if I did not look so "black"? What would my experiences have been if I were mixed with white? Would people still have assumed that I was smart because I was Japanese if I were Asian and white?

People of multiracial backgrounds have been used throughout history to create and recreate racial categories, to give race meaning and to maintain racial hierarchy in the United States, and it is still happening today. Therefore, my research will analyze how the concept of race is given meaning on the macro and micro levels in order to try to understand how racial categories are constructed, and how racial hierarchies are established, maintained and enforced through the experiences of people of Asian/white and Asian/black backgrounds.

Statement of the Problem

This study is an effort to pull current public discourse and the majority of academic research regarding multiracial people away from treating race in the same manner as ethnicity (Fulbeck 2006; Gaskins 1999; Root 1996). Thinking that one's race can be discarded by a given individual or absorbed into mainstream culture, as is assumed with European ethnicities, allows an understanding of racial identity as an issue of choice and assumes that increased intermarriage signifies acceptance through marital assimilation. However, what this paradigm does not acknowledge is that the assimilation process has been indelibly shaped through the concept of race because of the social constraints it imposes on these choices in our everyday lives.

My investigation focuses primarily on how people of Asian/white and Asian/black backgrounds experience race in their everyday lives, and will undergo the process of uncovering how the white/black continuum affects how they were socialized into understanding what race means. Examining the lived lives of people of multiple racial backgrounds allows us to understand the complex nature of how race is socially constructed, broadens current understanding of theories concerning race and sheds light on how discourse regarding multiracial people functions as a racial project that promotes, enforces and perpetuates essentialist notions of race and racial hierarchy through its focus on identity rather than racial justice.

This research examines, questions and confronts three of the most often assumed outcomes of an increasingly multiracial society. First, is the idea that the increase of people of multiracial heritage will eventually result in the discontinued use of racial categories (Gilroy

2003; Zack 1993). Although the number of children of multiracial heritage is increasing (Williams-Leon and Nakashima 2001), what will be observed is how racial categories are actually further reified through discourse surrounding people of multiple racial backgrounds, both by the multiracial person and through social interaction with family, friends and others.

Second, is that people of multiracial backgrounds will personally challenge racial categories and use their personal experiences to contradict race and racism (Brunsma 2006; Root 1996; Zack 1993). This idea comes from the understanding that the multiracial movement is largely, if not solely, an issue of identity. However, what this study will bring to the forefront is how the personal identities of people of multiracial backgrounds follow distinctly racial patterns that ultimately privilege whiteness and devalue blackness. In other words, the development of an identity is primarily *racial* in its composition, as multiracial people continuously assign, assess and evaluate their attitudes, aptitudes and abilities in a profoundly racial, and many times racist, manner.

And lastly, is the public notion that multiracial people will experience less racism, i.e., gain greater social acceptance, and live lives that are less constrained by race because of their "ambiguous" phenotypes (DaCosta 2006; Guevarra 2003; Streeter 1996; Hollinger 1995), or because their racial make-up allows them to be "bridges" between their racial communities (Rockquemore et al. 2009), and/or they represent the best of both worlds (Hall and Trude 2001; Hall 1996; Hall 1992). Currently, the best example of this public opinion is Tiger Woods, whose meteoric rise in the world of advertising was about his skill at golf *and* his multiracial background (DaCosta 2006). However, again this research will expose the seeming lack of hesitation by society to "fit" people of multiracial backgrounds into mono-racial categories, and therefore, discriminate against them according to their own ideologies, and also how Asian and black people often discriminate against people of multiracial backgrounds because of their assumed lack of authenticity.

Another related emphasis of this research is to address the assumption that an increase in interracial families signifies the breakdown of racist ideology in general and towards the interracially married groups specifically (Williams-Leon and Nakashima 2001; Patterson 1997). Although this is a common belief, an examination of Asian and white and Asian and black interracial families reveals two main findings: one, that people in interracial marriages in general, but interracially married black couples specifically, get married *despite* the racial animosity between the races, not because they have lessened; and two, that race and racism are central ideologies that continue to operate in the lives of interracially married couples, and how they socialize their children regarding what races are acceptable marriage partners. Interracially married Asian and white couples impose a "do as I say, not as I do" philosophy regarding their children's choice in marriage partners that pressures their children to marry people from socially acceptable racial groups. Also, it will be demonstrated that interracially married Asian and white couples teach their children that black people are the most undesirable marriage partners, therefore, privileging whiteness and maintaining white supremacy. Interracially married Asian and black couples also reinforce the color line by teaching their children to be aware of how people from other races may not think of black people as acceptable marriage partners.

Methodology

Why Asian/White and Asian/Black People?

This study focused on people of Asian/white and Asian/black backgrounds because of several factors. First, the relative size of the mixed-race Asian population cannot be numerically understated. In the 1990 U.S. Census, the reported number of children from interracial households was 1,037,420, and nearly half of those children, 466,590, were in families that marked one parent as Asian and the other parent as white (Williams-Leon and Nakashima 2001). This number was even more astounding when I considered the fact that Asian Americans only make up 3 percent of the U.S. population, and that multiracial Asian/black people were not considered in the final number.

Second, many multiracial activists, authors and scholars suggested that the experiences of minority/minority mixed-race individuals may be substantially different than those of white/minority heritage, and that much research was needed in this area (Hall 2001; Thornton and Gates 2001; Hall 1996; Hollinger 1993; Kich 1992; Omi 2001; Omi and Winant 1996; Root 2001; Root 1992; Williams 1992; Waters 1990). Although some research was done directly regarding people of minority/minority heritage (Thornton and Gates 2001; Comas-Diaz 1996; Hall 1992; Thornton 1992), these studies primarily focus on mental health and identity issues rather than racial experiences. The little research that was conducted using people of Asian/white and Asian/black backgrounds also focused on ethnic identification (Hall

2001; Williams 1992), rather than exploring how these two groups experience race in their everyday lives, and how those experiences may privilege whiteness.

And lastly, this study focused on people of Asian/white and Asian/black backgrounds because it allowed the creation of a theoretical framework for understanding how people of multiracial backgrounds experience race that recognized issues of power, especially as it pertained to white supremacy (Omi 2001; Winant 2001). Although studies mentioned how being of Asian/white or Asian/black background could make a difference in how one chooses an ethnic identity (Hall 2001; Williams 1992), it was important to note that these projects did not develop how those choices were restricted, at best, and forced, at worst, because of the privileging of white racial mixture over black.

Who Did I Interview?

In this research I have interviewed a total of thirty-two respondents of Asian/White and Asian/Black parentage with one parent identifying as Asian[1], and the other parent identifying as either white or black[2]. I also interviewed six sets of interracial parents, three with a white spouse and three with a black spouse in order to add context to the responses of the multiracial people I interviewed. Because of the intricacies of sampling this population, a snowball sampling method was used to generate my sample by using my initial social contacts first, and once interviewed, asking them if they knew anyone else that I could interview who fit my research (See *Appendix A*).

In-depth interviews with basic demographic, open-ended and Likert-scale questions were used in order to develop a theoretical framework that gave greater understanding of how people of Asian/white and Asian/black backgrounds experienced race in their everyday lives. Basic demographic questions included variables such as age, parent's birth country and whether they ever lived in their foreign parent's birth country. Open-ended questions asked how the respondent identified themselves racially, and what their basic social relationships were with other racial and social groups. The Likert-scale questions pertained to how the respondent felt they and others perceived their race, what racial groups did they feel accepted by and how much did they identify with their parents' racial groups (See *Appendix B*). Questions for the parents were similar to those asked of people of multiracial backgrounds (See *Appendix C*). These questions sought to gain a deeper understanding of the influences that institutions, social location, family, perceived acceptance/rejection and social understandings of race have on people of multiracial backgrounds.

Social Demographics of Sample

Of the thirty-two participants, sixteen people of Asian/white and sixteen people of Asian/black backgrounds were represented in this study. The even recruitment of people of Asian/white and Asian/black backgrounds was not meant to be understood as a representative sample, for people who are Asian/white by far exceeded the number of Asian/black people (Hall and Turner 2001; Williams-Leon and Nakashima 2001). However, since this study attempted to analyze the differences of how a multiracial Asian person of white or black background experiences race, it was necessary to oversample people of Asian/black backgrounds in order to make meaningful comparisons between these two populations.

Providing the demographic information of my group is not an effort to make general statements; it is an effort to give the reader a ready context to help understand the various social situations that the people in my sample may have experienced. The average age of my sample was twenty-nine years old, but my Asian/white group was considerably younger on average (24.6 years old) than the Asian/black group (33.8 years old). Of my sample, twenty-three respondents were born in the United States, while seventeen visited and twelve lived in their foreign parent's homeland. Twenty-six people had foreign-born mothers, and races of the mothers were as follows: three white, one black, fifteen Japanese, two Chinese and nine Filipino.

Twenty-four people had a father in the military, with twenty-seven total fathers being born in the United States. This was expected given that I drew my sample from San Diego County, which has two large military bases within its borders. I did ask which parent was in the military, but all the responses were that the father was the one in the military. The identified branches for fathers were as follows: fifteen Marine Corps, six Navy, one Army and one Air Force. This breakdown makes more sense given that the largest Marine Corp base, Camp Pendleton, is located in Northern San Diego County. The racial breakdown for fathers was: eleven white, fifteen black, two Japanese, one Chinese and one other Asian.

Participants were also recruited evenly in accordance to gender so that there would be eight men and eight women in each group. The even gender distribution was in response to literature that strongly suggested that being male or female may affect how a person of diverse racial background experiences race (Allman 1996; Comas-Diaz 1996; Hall

1992; Hall and Turner 2001; Root 1992; Root 2001; Streeter 1996; Valverde 2001; Williams 1992). Lastly, all respondents were at least eighteen years old in order to try and eliminate the trials of adolescence from this project (Hall 1992; Thornton and Gates 2001).

In summary, although I focus on the experiences of Asian/white and Asian/black people, these two groups are not the focus of my study. What I argue throughout my research is that people of Asian/white and Asian/black backgrounds provide a clearer lens to investigate the inter-workings of the concept of race, and, therefore, allow us to better theorize this construct. However, before I can go into more detail regarding the elements of this theoretical framework, we must first establish what race is and how this understanding has affected the manner in which we interpret people of diverse racial backgrounds.

Approaching Race

What is Race?

Race, gender and class are all socially constructed phenomena, which means that categories are defined, given meaning, enforced, changed, destroyed and recreated through human social interaction (Ore 2006; Lopez 2003). However, race is inherently different than gender and class because of the lack of objective, scientifically valid ways to measure racial categories (Lao et al. 2006; Fine et al. 2005; Commas 1961), while the social differences that exist between other groups are objective, scientifically quantifiable and irreducible to other social phenomena (Lipsitz 1998; Nash 1997; Lopez 1996; Oliver and Shapiro 1995; Omi and Winant 1994; Spickard 1992; Thornton 1992). Although the meanings of gender and class are highly subjective, can change dramatically from location to location and can be spatially located within a place as small as a household or as broad as a nation, the social construction of gender starts with the biological distinction between the sexes, while class distinctions are centered on who has more access to valued resources (Lorber 2006; Gilbert 1998; Omi and Winant 1994).

The incongruence between the lack of objective measure for racial categories and the persistence of the social effect of race have created the belief in many social scientists that race is somehow not real (Loveman 1999; Patterson 1997) and/or must be a manifestation or driven by other social constructs, namely class (Jung 2003; Wilson 1978). However, the paradox of the prevalence of race does not call for the abandonment of the concept of race, but a definition that can adequately explain the seeming inconsistency. In order to accomplish this task, I will first develop a socio-historical perspective of the concept of race, and then apply that context to the definition that I will develop as a result of this analysis.

The Beginnings of Race

The word "race" was first used in sixteenth century Europe and was based on kinship relationships and ancestry rather than physical characteristics, e.g., skin color (Feagin and Feagin 1999). The focus on heritage most likely occurred because of the lack of concrete and consistent physical distinctions between European peoples. The British and the Irish are excellent examples of this, as both groups would be considered "white" in the United States, but in Europe there exists a rigid hierarchy between these two groups that is believed to be biological in nature (Kennedy 2000; Roediger 1991).

Although physical dissimilarity does not manifest itself in the first usages of race, it is clear that some type of cultural distinction is necessary in order to fully actuate the concept of race through an analysis of English clothing laws. In *Channels of Desire*, Stuart and Elizabeth Ewen clearly demonstrate that clothes not only distinguished classes because of the unaffordability of lavish outfits, but also that these garments served as symbols of domination because the legal dress codes that determined social class were publicly and corporally enforced:

> No apprentice whatsoever should presume ... to wear (1) any clothing except what he received from his master; (2) a hat, or anything except a woolen cap ... (3) ruffles, cuffs, loose collars ... (4) anything except canvas, fustian [a stout fabric of cotton and flax], sack cloth, English leather, or woolen doublets, without any silver or silk trimming. Punishment for violation of the statute was at the discretion of the master for a first offense; a public whipping for a second offense; and six months added to the period of indenture for the third offense. (Ewen and Ewen 1992, p. 87)

This punishment is very similar to the punishment carried out against people who married across the color line in the United States. "Punishments for violating anti-miscegenation laws included enslavement, exile, whippings, fines, and imprisonment. Some jurisdictions punished those who performed such marriages" (Kennedy 2000, p. 145). This strongly suggests that by connecting the punishments to the crimes, one can also connect the crimes to the socially constructed categories.

Although Europeans may get credit for using the word "race" first, the concept is global and does not depend on European influence or context in order to establish. This can be demonstrated with a brief examination of the Eta in Japan.

The Eta

The origins of the Eta are unknown, but the two prevailing theories are that they are an outcast group of people of historically Hindu, Korean or Chinese descent who worked the dirty jobs of Japanese society, i.e., tanning and butchery, both of which were looked down upon by the Buddhist religion (Donoghue 1957). Although not physically distinct to an outsider from the rest of the Japanese population, the Eta people are an egregiously socially, economically, politically and religiously oppressed group that is constructed to be biologically distinct and genetically inferior to Japanese people:

> In such reports the Eta were generally referred to as being biologically inferior and inherently criminal, and anti-social acts in which they were involved were exaggerated, headlined, and given prominence in news reports. (Smythe and Naitoh 1953, p. 25)

So close in likeness are the Eta to the Japanese that laws were passed that established a dress code and hairstyle for the Eta people (Smythe and Naitoh 1953).

Although being associated with dirty jobs resulted in negative stereotypes of this group as innately "dirty," the evidence of a racial project is clearly illustrated by their treatment within the social and legal institutions of Japan. In reading the history of the Eta, one cannot help but to make the connection to black people in the United States and Jim Crow laws. The Eta were seen as less than human, or one-seventh of one ordinary Japanese:

> In one recorded instance in which a non-Eta killed an Eta, the judge ruled that punishment against the accused could not be carried out until at least seven Eta had been killed by the defendant, since the life of one ordinary Japanese was equal to the lives of seven Eta. (Smythe and Naitoh 1953, p. 22)

The Eta were considered biologically distinct and inferior to the point of creating anti-miscegenation laws and the producing of an ideology that stated that one would be unhappy and one's children would suffer severe physical and mental illnesses if one were to intermarry with them (Donoghue 1957).

Although officially freed August 28, 1871, the social construction of the Eta as an inferior biological group led to discrimination in school, work, politics and housing; however, this ill treatment paved the way for resistance by the Eta that is highly reflective of how black people and other Americans fought for Civil Rights:

> As a result of this organized effort, violence ensued in several parts of the country as the Eta attempted to enter public bath houses and other public places, demanding equal treatment and to insist on fairness to their children in public schools. (Smythe and Naitoh 1953, p. 27)

Therefore, to move to a sociology of group making would include global situations such as the Eta, but also acknowledge that these groupings are racial constructs in their truest form. Given this understanding, a definition of race must address how heredity forms the basis of the ideology that justifies the social inequality existing between groups.

The Social Construction of Race

It is with this understanding that I propose that race is a forced socially, historically and geographically-based concept where differential social statuses are constructed to be understood as hereditarily distinct groupings, and are arbitrarily assigned cultural/physical differences to identify and justify the social inequalities that exist between these groups. Although modern understandings of race coincide with visible physical characteristics, race is not as much about physical distinctions as it is determining a person's social status through heritage. Physical distinctions are only as important as they are consistent with socially constructed understandings of what is an essential characteristic of a specific race, e.g., skin color, hair texture. However, if how one looks to others is not consistent with the heritage of their parents, then their heritage, not their phenotype, is used to determine their social location.

Once it becomes demonstrated that race is a social construction, it becomes important to describe how this is accomplished. The prevailing discourse in the social sciences suggests that race is a social construction devoid of any predetermined and inherent biological meaning (Lipsitz 1998; Nash 1997; Lopez 1996; Spickard 1992; Thornton 1992).

Understanding race in this manner allows us to connect how macro and micro-level forces give meaning to racial categories by assigning social consequences to these groupings.

Race on a Macro-level

The concept of race begins its official recognition within the United States Constitution and is immediately and inseparably linked to racial hierarchy through the establishment of the Three-Fifths Compromise that states that slaves should be counted as three-fifths of a person (Mezey 2003; Snipp 2003). Not only was racial hierarchy established, but racial stratification soon followed, as advantages and privileges were given to people who were determined to be white. In no place is this clearer than in the 1790 Naturalization Act, which stated that only "free, white persons" could become naturalized citizens of the United States, which allowed whites the advantage of citizenship, the accumulation of wealth and equality under the law (McGoveny 2003; Lopez 1996; Fong 1971).

These objective, quantifiable advantages that whites have in comparison to non-whites have created what George Lipsitz calls a "possessive investment in whiteness" where:

> Whiteness has a cash value: it accounts for advantages that come to individuals through profits made from housing secured in discriminatory markets, through the unequal educations allocated to children of different races, through insider networks that channel employment opportunities to the relatives and friends of those who have profited most from present and past racial discrimination, and especially through intergenerational transfers of inherited wealth that pass on the spoils of discrimination to succeeding generations. (Lipsitz 1998, p. vii)

Whiteness gives distinct advantages in the accumulation and transfer of wealth (Oliver and Shapiro 1995), housing (Lipsitz 1998), jobs (Wilson 1996), education (Kozol 2006; Steinberg 1995), the justice system (Cole 2006) and politics (Saito 1998). Linking these discrepancies to the concept of race is where many social scientists stop in regards to demonstrating how race is socially constructed. However, what this represents is not what race *is*, but what the consequences of race *are*, and does not adequately challenge how racial categories are formed in the first place.

Therefore, the social construction of race does not start with the differential social rewards assigned to these groups, but in the actual construction of them. In other words, who is white? Who is black? Who are Native Americans and Asians? And where do these groups fit in the racial hierarchy? These are the questions that begin the social construction process, and are clearly evidenced through a sociohistorical analysis of the U.S. Census and the legal system.

The U.S. Census
How we conceive of race creates the context for racism, and the U.S. Census has played a central role in informing society of who is of what race. This construction informs us as to who deserves what resources. The need for the census arose out of the creation of distinct subordinate groups in the United States Constitution—Indians and slaves—and our need to count them (Mezey 2003). Although racial characteristics were always used as an indicator for one's legal and political status, these characteristics were explicitly introduced in 1820 when the term "color" was added to the census (Snipp 2003). Even though racial categories are themselves socially constructed in numerous ways, I will focus on how multiracial people of black/white heritage were counted in the census to demonstrate how this concept works.

Interestingly enough, it was during and immediately after slavery when people of multiracial black/white heritage were counted in the census. 1850 marked the first year mulattos were counted, with 1890 adding the categories of quadroon and octoroon, people of one-quarter and one-eighth black heritage respectively (Snipp 2003; Mezey 2003). During this time period, many people of black/white heritage had an intermediate social position between that of white and black, with the most notable group being the Creoles, a group mixed with black, French and Spanish heritage where some even owned slaves (Borders 1988).

Unlike Indians and blacks, there was no legal or constitutional reason to count mulattos besides their being so prolific on the American landscape, which was also the main reason the Chinese were counted in California (Menzy 2003). The counting of mulattos reveals how racial categories are socially constructed to the forefront, as enumerators were instructed to use social status as a key to interpreting a person's racial category if they were physically ambiguous (Snipp 2003). What this means is that a person could be white, if and only if, they were of the status of whites, in other words, free. While if you looked white, but were a slave, then you were obviously black. Understanding the connection between color and status ushered in the concept of passing, where a person that would be socially considered black passes as white (Daniel 1992).

The social construction of race goes to a new level as one considers how racial categories are affected by location. This is demonstrated by the fact that the counts of Native Americans were reasonably accurate in areas where people from this group were concentrated, but Native Americans were dramatically undercounted in city environments because of the inability of enumerators to identify them where concentrations were low (Snipp 2003). The association between location and race was also taken advantage of by brown-skinned mulattos who gave themselves Spanish surnames and then moved to areas that had a high population of Mexican Americans (Davis 1991). Understanding the relationship between race and location allows Ian F. Haney Lopez to state, "While housing patterns and citizenship have depended on race, the converse is true as well: race often follows from neighborhoods and nationality" (Lopez 1996, p. 120).

Race and the Legal System
Although a significant amount of history happened within these seventy years, two significant events led to the subsuming of people of black/white backgrounds within a black racial classification: Jim Crow laws and the establishment of race as common sense. Immediately after the end of the Reconstruction period, a time when people of African heritage experienced unprecedented social, economic and political gains, white southerners created Jim Crow laws that were designed to re-subjugate black people (Davis 1991). The creation of these laws demanded a definition for who was considered black, which led to the legal institution of the "one drop rule."

Nowhere was the creation of this rule more necessary than in the enforcement of anti-miscegenation laws, as many states tried to enforce fractional amounts of black heritage, but ultimately accepted the "one drop rule" to enforce the boundaries between the races (Hickman 2003). By instituting this rule, counting people of black/white heritage as anything other than black became superfluous, thus leading to the dropping of all multiracial categories from the U.S. Census by the year 1920 (Snipp 2003).

Although Jim Crow laws forced the legal system to reify racial categories through the "one drop rule," when pseudo-scientific means to discern between the races began to breakdown, the court played another key role by establishing what is now the primary criteria for which the races will be based on: common sense. In his book, *White By Law*, Ian F. Haney Lopez clearly demonstrates the legal transition from understanding race as biology to understanding race as common sense. In *Ozawa v. United States*, the U.S. Supreme Court established that

Japanese were not white because the term "white persons" only pertained to people who were commonly understood as being of the Caucasian race (Lopez 1996, p. 79). However, just three months later in the case of *United States v. Thind* involving Asian Indians who are scientifically classified as Caucasian, the Court completely backed off of a scientific understanding of race and made common sense the sole criteria for judging whiteness (Ibid.). However, as will be argued later, racial common sense is also breaking down as people are becoming increasingly aware of their multiracial backgrounds, thus ushering in the need for "racial logic" to determine the race of a person.

Race on a Micro-level

Ironically, the same instrument (the U.S. Census) that is largely responsible for creating a macro-level understanding of race is also responsible, to what degree is debatable, in creating the battleground regarding how race would be experienced on a micro-level. This occurred in 1960, when the Census Bureau switched from enumerators to self-identification to obtain racial statistics (Mezey 2003).

On the surface, having people self-identify their race does not seem all that significant, but in order to make this happen two ideological shifts had to occur. First, is that race was not as much about physical difference as it was about cultural affinity (Snipp 2003). But second, and most important, the common sense of race had to be socially, politically, legally and economically established well enough in our society so that race would now become a part of personal identity regardless of physical appearance. Understanding the shift from enumerators to self-identification allows us to connect how the U.S. Census became the focus of people of multiracial backgrounds and the parents of multiracial children regarding their political platform.

In 1977, the Office of Management and Budget (OMB) issued Directive 15, which gave the U.S. Census its primary racial categories; shortly afterwards, advocacy for a multiracial category started as early as 1988 (Snipp 2003; Spencer 1999). Two groups, the Association of Multi-Ethnic Americans (AMEA) and Project RACE (Reclassify All Children Equally) took the lead regarding the creation of a multiracial category, and in 1997, partially succeeded by having the U.S. Census allow people to select more than one racial category to define their heritage (Mezey 2003).

The reason for considering the "check all that apply" configuration a partial victory was that neither group had originally advocated for a "mark all that apply" option. Although Project RACE did do substantial foundational work regarding the combined format, they initially proposed a stand-alone multiracial category, while AMEA advocated for a separate multiracial category with racial designations (Spencer 1999). While the implications for each designation diverged on numerous levels, the unifying idea behind creating a multiracial category is that people of multiracial heritage all share a common racial experience. This assumption will be tested throughout my research as I compare and contrast the lived lives of people of Asian/white backgrounds to those of Asian/black backgrounds to see what experiences they have in common and those they do not.

An additional key assumption of these advocacy groups that will be challenged is the eventual outcome of including people of multiracial heritage on the census. Although AMEA is an advocacy group comprised of multiracial people and Project RACE is a group comprised mainly of parents of multiracial children, both groups believe, "... that a federal multiracial category will facilitate the dismantling of the American racial construct" (Ibid., p. 125). This belief is endorsed by David Hollinger who argues that multiracial people, especially those of Asian/white and Asian/black heritage, will eventually invalidate how we think of race in the United States because of our lack of history in dealing with these two groups (Hollinger 1995). However, this belief forms the foundation of another driving question of this research: Does the assertion of a multiracial identity amongst people of Asian/white and Asian/black backgrounds actually challenge the concept of race?

Theoretical Framework

Creating a theoretical framework for understanding the lived experiences of multiracial people begins with understanding their place within assimilation, the process of reducing boundaries between people from different social groups (Hwang, Saenz and Aguirre 1997), the essence of which is the formation of a unified nation unstratified and undivided by race and ethnicity (Jung 2003). Counter to the prevalent beliefs of the time that situated non-white people as unable to assimilate into the American mainstream (Fong 1971), Robert E. Park proposed a *race relations cycle* that would ultimately lead to the full incorporation of people of color: "The race relations cycle which takes the form, to state abstractly, of contacts, competition, accommodation and eventual assimilation, is apparently progressive and irreversible" (Park 1950, p. 150).

Milton Gordon furthered the race relations cycle by developing stages regarding assimilation, which addressed how to operationalize

Park's theory. Gordon proposed seven dimensions to assimilation: cultural assimilation (changing to core cultural values), structural assimilation (inclusion into primary social institutions), marital assimilation (significant intermarriage), identification assimilation (development of a sense of identity with mainstream society), attitude-receptional assimilation (absence of prejudice and stereotypes), behavior-receptional assimilation (absence of direct and indirect discrimination) and civic assimilation (absence of power conflict) (Gordon 1964). Although Parks believed assimilation to be a linear process, Gordon's conceptualization of assimilation does not necessitate that one stage must follow another, and suggests that some stages may pertain to a particular group while others may not (Hirschman 1983). Even though one stage is not dependent on another, marital assimilation is widely accepted as the culmination, the proverbial endpoint of the assimilation process (Hwang, Saenz and Aguirre 1997).

Understanding interracial marriage as the ultimate goal of assimilation makes multiracial children the living embodiment of the melting pot, where people of different ethnicities are forged together as one (Xie and Goyette 1997). However, if people of multiracial backgrounds are the endpoint of assimilation, then that should mean that they live lives that are completely integrated into mainstream America. It is this assumption that I will examine throughout my research as I analyze the lives of people of Asian/white and Asian/black backgrounds to measure the extent that they are assimilated into America.

How Race Affects Assimilation

To begin the analysis of people of Asian/white and Asian/black backgrounds, it must be recognized how the pervasive voice within current multiracial discourse is subsumed within an ethnicity framework. Understanding this compels us to ask the question: Is race the same as ethnicity? If not, what could the consequences of this assumption reveal in an analysis of people of Asian/white and Asian/black backgrounds?

Ethnicity is popularly defined as a group of people that are recognized by others and by themselves as being culturally distinct (Ore 2006). However, what clearly distinguishes ethnicity and race is how they are understood socially, which can be clearly demonstrated within the assimilation process and its three possible endpoints: Anglo conformity, the melting pot and cultural pluralism (Hirschman 1983; Feagin and Feagin 1999). Anglo conformity suggests that ethnicity is something that people are willing to give up in order to become part of the mainstream, but is race something a person can give up? The melting pot proposes that new ethnicities are absorbed and made a part of a new American ethnicity, but is race something that can be absorbed? Cultural pluralism implies that all levels of assimilation are obtained while remaining ethnic distinctions are considered equal, but can races ever be equal? Ethnicity and race both have a cultural component, but race is constructed as permanent, unabsorbable and inherently unequal. But the larger question of my research is to ask, is this true for all races?

Except Black People
In order to answer these questions, we must examine how racial categories are derived. It is clear that being black is defined by hypo-descent, better known in this context as the "one drop rule," where one drop of black blood makes a person black (Davis 1991), but what about the other races?

Interestingly enough, the amount of white heritage that a person of Native American ancestry was counted on the census because there was a need to construct a boundary to being considered Native American. This was done partially, if not entirely, due to the fact that the government wanted to limit their legal obligations to this particular group:

> Needless to say, hyperdescent was a convenient device for limiting the obligations from treaties and other agreements that had been incurred by the federal government throughout the preceding century. In the coming decades, the federal government would establish minimum blood quantum standards for being judged an authentic American Indian and hence being eligible for a variety of federal services, including education and health care. (Snipp 2003)

The construction of hyper-descent, the social practice of multiracial people identifying with the dominant rather than the subordinate group, among people of Native American backgrounds has directly led to people of white/Native American backgrounds having the highest probability of identifying as white in school, as compared to people of white/black and white/Asian backgrounds (Harris and Sim 2002).

This type of blood quantum rule is also found within the qualifications of the Cherry Blossom Beauty Pageants that happen in Japanese American communities, which state that a person has to be at least half Japanese in order to participate (King 2001). What this strongly suggests is that a person who is only one-quarter Japanese, with only one Asian grandparent amongst three white parents, would be considered white by the Japanese American community. This is further supported by the fact that there is not a single legal case involving the racial classification of a person of one-quarter Asian heritage (Lopez 1996).

However, what does black hypo-descent and Native American and Asian hyper-descent mean within the assimilation process? What it suggests is that every race, except black people, can eventually shed their race by intermarrying with white people. It proposes that every race, except black people, can eventually be absorbed by the surrounding white population. And it implies that every race, except black people, can eventually become equal to whites with the right amount of white mixture. Drawing the lines around whiteness and blackness in such a manner will be a central focus of my research as I examine whether being mixed with white or black makes a difference for people of Asian/white and Asian/black backgrounds as they experience race and the assimilation process.

The Multiracial Project

By treating race as the same as ethnicity, we are unable to explain differential patterns of assimilation amongst people of different racial groups (Omi and Winant 1994; Hirschman 1983). This revelation necessitates that we move multiracial discourse out of the ethnicity paradigm and center it within the racial formations process[3].

Michael Omi and Howard Winant define the concept of racial formations as, "the sociohistorical process by which racial categories are created, inhabited, transformed, and destroyed" (Omi and Winant 1994, p. 55). Acknowledging this transition then locates current multiracial discourse a racial project:

> ... is simultaneously an interpretation, representation, or explanation of racial dynamics, and an effort to reorganize and redistribute resources along particular racial lines. Racial projects connect what race means in a particular discursive practice and the ways in which both social structures and everyday experiences are racially organized, based upon that meaning. (Ibid., p. 56)

In other words, racial formations is the process in which racial projects connect social meaning to racial categories. By situating multiracial discourse as a racial project, my research will examine how racial dynamics are being reorganized around the subject of multiraciality among people of Asian/white and Asian/black backgrounds. What will be demonstrated throughout this study is how race organizes and structures the experiences of multiracial people; how essentialist notions of race are constructed, enforced and perpetuated in their lives by themselves and society; and how race slows, if not altogether stops the assimilation process.

Establishing Racial Logic

Although Omi and Winant state that racial projects connect what race means within a particular socio-historical setting, they do not create a mechanism to distinguish how racial categories are established. The racial formations process capriciously assigns unsubstantiated and implausible mental, physical, emotional and spiritual attributes to arbitrarily chosen hereditary differences that may manifest themselves culturally or physically; however, as the number of people who are aware and acknowledge their multiracial backgrounds increases, this becomes even harder to do. The differences between the races only gain meaning within the social structure of the United States during specific historical moments through the development of a racial "common sense" (Gilroy 2003; Hunt 1999; Lipsitz 1998; Lopez 1996). However, I will argue throughout my research that racial common sense is currently being rearticulated by the notion of "racial logic" as it changes our understanding of racial categories.

In his book, *White By Law*, Ian F. Haney Lopez clearly demonstrates the legal transition from understanding race as biology to understanding race as common sense. However, racial common sense is limited to presupposed meanings regarding specific monoracial categories, and is ill-equipped to handle newly acknowledged and never before encountered racial combinations presented by today's multiracial population.

These new combinations require "racial logic" to bring together existing common sense and develop a new understanding of people of multiracial backgrounds that will affect how their attitudes, aptitudes and abilities are interpreted, rationalized and compartmentalized, which centers on reconstructing their racial categorization. For example, if black people are supposed to be athletic, while Asians are supposed to be good at math, would an Asian/black person be athletic and good at math?

Therefore, by using "racial logic," it will be clearly demonstrated how the lived lives of the multiracial people in my sample are shaped by the institutions and organizations of society, and how their personal identity is formed along essentialist racial lines.

Perception as Reality

Lastly, I want to connect the Thomas theorem, which states that, "if men [sic] define situations as real, they are real in their consequences" (Thomas and Thomas 1928), to my analysis of the lived experiences of people of Asian/white and Asian/black backgrounds. I have already argued that race is not a real category of any biological significance; however, it is a real category based upon its social consequences. The use of this theorem allows me to focus on how the multiracial people and the parents of multiracial children in my sample experience race without essentializing the existence of racial categories. In other words, what they believe race to be is key to understanding how race operates in their lives, which is central to my analysis.

To think of race in such a way does not privilege micro-level experiences over macro-level structures; on the contrary, it complements them. How people of Asian/white and Asian/black backgrounds and their parents experience race in their daily lives, I will argue, form the basis of understanding how the concept of race operates on a societal level as well. Therefore, the use of this theorem allows me to develop how race is conceived, how race is socially constructed and how race is socially reproduced in the lives of multiracial people and their parents without assuming that races or racial categories exist independent of a racialized state.

It was with this framework in mind that facilitated the creation and ordering of the chapters of my research. Chapter 2: *Internal Racial Identity* will speak directly to the social processes that people are taught and use on an everyday basis in order to interpret and understand the concept of race. This chapter will focus on the seemingly ubiquitous "What are you?" question and examine its context against the actual physical appearance, social location and personal abilities of people of multiracial backgrounds. Chapter 3: *External Racial Identity* will consider the arguments of Mary Waters in her book, *Ethnic Options*, to try and ascertain whether race can be symbolic. This chapter will also discuss what factors facilitate acceptance into particular racial/ethnic/social groups, and whether this acceptance is affected by racial heritage. Chapter 4: *The External Context of Racial Identity Formation* looks into how people of Asian/white and Asian/black backgrounds experience racism in our society, and will compare the similarities and differences of being mixed with either white or black. Chapter 5: *Learning Racial Hierarchy* will seek to connect the lived lives of the parents with how their children experienced race and racism.

Notes

1. I use Asian, and not Asian American, because of this study's focus upon how people of diverse racial heritage experience race; not how they negotiate their cultural identity, which is the immediate connotation of Asian American.
2. Black is admittedly acknowledged as an inherently multiracial classification, while White is considered pure and unmixed (Davis 1991; Zack 1993). Therefore, this study will include participants with multiracial Black parents who are not immediately multiracial and/or do not have a multiracial consciousness.
3. Although some would argue that the multiracial movement gains its strength to question the construction of race due to its pan-Asian construction (Hollinger 1995), which suggests that a pan-ethnicity model may be more appropriate (Spencer 1999; Espiritu 1992), I would argue that this movement's strength is actually situated in its whiteness (Parker and Song 2001), which strongly suggests a racial formations framework (Omi and Winant 1994).

2
Internal Racial Identity

What is a racial identity? Roger Brubaker and Fredrick Cooper (2000) speak to the seeming contradiction of developing an operational definition of identity that allows for fluidity, but still can address "essentialist" movements:

> We argue that the prevailing constructivist stance on identity—the attempt to "soften" the term, to acquit it of the charge of "essentialism" by stipulating that identities are constructed, fluid, and multiple—leaves us without a rationale for talking about "identities" at all and ill-equipped to examine the "hard" dynamics and essentialist claims of contemporary identity politics. (Brubaker and Cooper 2000, p. 1)

Although the authors suggest that the manner to bypass this paradox is by conceptualizing identity as simultaneously a category of practice (soft) and a category of analysis (hard), I argue that the inability to separate "soft" and "hard" identities is the result of the conflation of a cultural identity with a racial identity.

Walter Benn Michaels (1994) addresses the difference between cultural identity and racial identity by examining the ubiquitous case of Susie Guillory Phipps. The author states that Phipps' cultural identity should be white because she had always thought of herself as white and had married twice as white, but that her racial identity was determined by the court as "colored":

> "Individual racial designations are purely social and cultural perceptions", the court said; the relevant question, then, was not whether those perceptions correctly registered some scientific fact (since the court denied there was any relevant scientific fact) but

whether they had been "correctly recorded" at the time the birth certificate was issued. Since in the court's judgment they had been, Phipps and her fellow appellants remained "colored." (Michaels 1994, p. 764)

With this understanding, Michaels strongly criticizes the desire of constructivists to replace racial identity with cultural identity because of the fundamental difference in how they are used in our society:

> I criticize the idea of antiessentialist accounts of identity, which is to say that I criticize in particular the idea of cultural identity as a replacement for racial identity. My central point is that for the idea of cultural identity to do any work beyond describing the beliefs people actually hold and the things they actually do, it must resort to some version of the essentialism it begins by repudiating ... For insofar as your culture no longer consists in the things you actually do and believe, it requires some link between you and your culture that transcends practice. That link, I argue, has, in the United States, characteristically been provided by race. (Michaels 1994, p. 758)

In other words, cultural identity is tied to the things that people do and can be fluid, but racial identity is a constrained, if not altogether forced, identification that implies an essence that a person has or does not have. Michaels' conceptualization strongly implies that racial identities are fixed along a white/black continuum, but does this also apply to Asian/white and Asian/black people?

Understanding how cultural identity and racial identity are assumed to be the same thing is the key that connects current multiracial literature to identity politics. Pearl Fuyo Gaskins, in her book, *What are you? Voices of Mixed-Race Young People*, used her book to explore the meaning of race and how racial identities were constructed. Her work used poetry, photographs, essays and interviews with people of multiracial backgrounds to give voice to a movement that had been long in the making. Gaskins focused her attention on the lived experiences of people of multiracial backgrounds by addressing the ubiquitous question that all multiracial people seem to have faced at one time or another, and in one form or another: "What are you?" The encountering of this question was also true with all thirty-two people that I interviewed.

While powerful and thought-provoking in the manner in which it was handled, equating cultural identity to racial identity limits understanding of the lived lives of multiracial people because of its inability to connect the "What are you?" question to racialized social structures. Because of this, the multiracial project only addresses why multiracial people are asked this question on an individualistic basis, rather than linking it to how we understand race on a societal level. In other words, rather than solely focusing on a multiracial person's response to this question, my research will place the responses within a racial formations framework.

The Fluidity of Identity

The fluidity of identity can be seen in Mary C. Waters book, *Ethnic Options*, which examines the effects of assimilation on the ethnic identity of whites of European heritage that were of the Roman Catholic faith. Although assimilation theories suggest that the decrease of structural forces, e.g., residential segregation and interethnic marriage, would result in the casting away of one's ethnic identity in favor of a more universal "American" identity, what Waters uncovers in her research is that a majority of later-generation white people still identify with an ethnic group. Although some would argue that the claiming of an Irish ethnicity is non-problematic (Greenberg 1999; Mulderink 1996), Waters maintains that white ethnicity is highly symbolic in nature, suggesting that white ethnic identification is largely a leisure or recreational activity with no real social consequences, e.g. wearing green on St. Patrick's Day. "In other words, for later-generation white ethnics, ethnicity is not something that influences their lives unless they *want* it to (emphasis in the original)" (Waters, 1990, p.7).

Waters' focus on white ethnics begs the question as to whether multiracial people would somehow use their backgrounds in a symbolic manner. This is a question that she suggests herself in her concluding remarks, and states that what is flexible, symbolic or voluntary for middle-class whites may not be so for people of color:

> For the ways in which ethnicity is flexible and symbolic and voluntary for white middle-class Americans are the very ways in which it is not so for non-white and Hispanic Americans. Thus the discussions of the influence of looks and surname on ethnic choice would look very different if one were describing a person who was one-quarter Italian and three quarters African American or a woman whose married name changed from O'Connell to Martinez. The social and political consequences of being Asian or Hispanic or black are not symbolic for the most part, or voluntary. They are real and often hurtful. (156)

Although considerate of racial dynamics, Waters does not adequately explain *why* she should expect multiracial people to act any differently than multiethnic whites if people of multiracial heritage are experiencing much of the same destructualization that interethnic whites have experienced. So the driving question of this chapter becomes: Is the racial identity of people of Asian/white and Asian/black backgrounds something they can treat in a symbolic manner?

Assimilation and Racial Identity

Building upon the work of David Harris and Jeremiah Sim regarding racial identities amongst multiracial people, I will use their framework of internal, external and expressed racial identities to analyze the experiences of people of Asian/white and Asian/black heritage. Internal racial identities are what an individual believes about their own race, external racial identities are what others think of the multiracial person's race, and expressed racial identities, which I will use interchangeably with cultural identity, are the words and actions that convey beliefs about a multiracial person's race (Harris and Sim 2002). In this chapter, I will focus on internal racial identities, and then develop external and expressed racial identities in the next chapter.

Although presented as separate analytical spaces, the authors acknowledge how these identities may influence each other in a convoluted, complicated and even contradictory manner. Adding to the racial identity literature, I will argue throughout this chapter that the development of a racial identity, one that is biologically understood and socially enforced, is, at best, inconsistent, and, at worst, contradictory to an assimilationist framework because of the inherit hierarchy between the races. It will also be argued through the next three chapters that if the assimilation process is applicable to racial categories, then as the "Americanization" process unfolds, there should be evidence of a converging racial identity towards Anglo-conformity or a melting pot identity (Hirschman 1983).

(Re)Creating Racial Categories and the Establishment of Racial Logic

Although the essence of the "What are you?" question is to figure out a person's race, understanding this concept within a racial formations framework uncovers the deeper meaning behind this question: the desire of the person asking the question to apply "racial logic" to the multiracial person in order to figure out where they fit within the racial hierarchy. Racial logic builds upon what is currently understood as racial common sense, which *gives* meaning to racial categories (Hunt 1999; Lipsitz 1998; Lopez 1996; Omi and Winant 1994); however, racial logic is the mechanism by which we construct the categories themselves. Racial logic is necessary in order to bring together existing common sense and develop a new understanding of people of multiracial backgrounds; how they should be seen, how they should be interpreted, how they should be categorized and, most importantly, how they should be treated. Therefore, this chapter will explore the hidden, or not so hidden, meaning behind why the people in my sample are asked the "What are you?" question, and how this question is rooted in how race is reified, (re)interpreted and (re)enforced through the everyday interactions of people of the Asian/white and Asian/black backgrounds in my study.

The "What are You?" Question and the Application of Racial Logic

Every person that I interviewed was asked a variation of what they were at differing times in a given relationship and with varying levels of frequency. Race is primarily, if not solely, understood as a public display (Hunt 1999; S. Hall 1997); however, if a person is in anyway ambiguous in their phenotype, there are multiple ways to try and identify a person's race. The most direct manner to discover someone's race is to ask them, which is what Margaret has to deal with on a daily basis as people struggle with her external racial identity. This struggle becomes evident as she is asked by complete strangers without a proper introduction what she is:

> **Margaret (abf[1] 46)** – Yes, they stop me in the street. People I don't even know asked me ... I'll be in a store and people ask me all the time what my nationality is constantly. People ask me all the time and it's a little disturbing. It's really strange; if other people walk down the street, do people ask them if they're Irish Italian? (laughs) But when I walk down the street I warrant everyone asking me what nationality I am.

This statement clearly situates Margaret's understanding of race as equivalent to ethnicity, as she equates being asked about her race to a person being asked if they are "Irish Italian." Perhaps understanding race as ethnicity makes her believe that being asked about her race is "strange," because a person's ethnicity is not always on display, nor is it of any major concern when one is regarded as white (Waters 1990).

However, understanding that the roots of this question are rooted in how racial categories are socially constructed allows the frequent "What are you?" questions to be connected to her racial ambiguity. This connection is strongly supported by Gaskins' (1999) work, as the people in her sample continuously faced people who were not sure of what race the multiracial person in question was, to the point where this question became the foundation for a multiracial identity.

Thinking of race as ethnicity is made easy because people are asking Margaret what her nationality is, rather than asking directly about her race. However, it becomes clear that people want to know her race when I asked her why she believes people question her so often:

> **Margaret (abf 46)** – It's because no one can figure out what I am. (laughs) I don't look black. If anything, Asian people tend to think I'm some type of Asian, like Filipinos think I'm Filipino. Now that I'm thinking about it, Hispanics might think I'm Hispanic. No one can figure me out, and my mom is laughing in the background when I said that. (laughs).

The statement that "no one can figure out what I am," begs the question as to why people need to figure out what she *is* in the first place? This is another recurring theme in the work of Gaskins, as people of multiracial heritage in her sample are quoted as wondering why their racial designation is the business of other people in the first place. Part of the solution may lie in the idea that racial minorities try to find/identify people of their own racial category, which would help in explaining why Filipinos think that Margaret is Filipino and Hispanics think that she is Hispanic. It also could be that people of these particular racial groups have a far broader range regarding how people of their particular race look.

However, I argue that this quote actually describes how racial categories are socially constructed, as her "What are you?" experiences announce how other people are using racial logic in order to figure out her race rather than her nationality or ethnicity. Since race is read off of the body, what Margaret is experiencing is people's angst over her racial ambiguity not her expressed identity, which in her case is American.

For Sabrina, the context of the "What are you?" question usually happens while she works at a hair salon:

> **Sabrina (awf[2] 49)** – It's mainly in my business; I work at a hair salon and we see people all the time. When I do their hair, we talk and ask where are you from? And I would say guess. (laughs) I usually tell them to guess, and they say Hawaiian but never

Okinawan or American ... I'm okay with it. I've pretty much been asked that my whole life.

Although Sabrina has come to accept this question as a part of her life, I was left wondering, why? Why would people ask her this question in her workspace? Is there a racial connection to be made? Perhaps it is because of the common practice for people to have their hair cut by people of the same race or ethnicity that prompts this question in this space? I wonder if her customers were uncomfortable with having someone that they could not racially identify cutting their hair, and if there was an answer that they would have considered unacceptable?

Something else that deserves more attention regarding how racial categories are socially constructed by people guessing Sabrina's race is the fact that they never guessed her as American. Maybe this was assumed within the framework of her being guessed as Hawaiian; however, I find it much more likely that her customers more readily identify being American with being white. Therefore, since Sabrina does not look "white" then she must be "foreign."

Connecting Racial Identity to Biology

Partially because of the multiracial project's ability to develop multiracial role models for today's multiracial people, e.g., Tiger Woods, Derrick Jeter, Mariah Carey, Prince and Jay-Z to name a few, when asked the question, "How do you identify yourself racially?" twenty-two of thirty-two respondents reported an internal multiracial identity. "Biology" was clearly taken into consideration as multiracial respondents explained why they stated their heritage on the second most intrusive manner of soliciting racial information to their internal racial identity: government forms.

For Patty and John, notions of their internal racial identities are rooted so deeply in biology that they are offended when government forms state to choose only one of their races for identification purposes:

>**Patty (awf 35)** – I'm Japanese and American. I am part of my mom and part of my dad. Putting it down on that paper makes me have to choose between them. I'd rather just leave it blank because I'm part of both of them.

>**John (abm[3] 33)** – When I identify myself racially sometimes I get offended because they tell me I can only pick one, but then I tell them that I'm black and Filipino. If I were to only say one I would feel discriminated, so I tell them I'm black and Filipino.

The socialization to biological claims to both heritages leads to a certain level of civil disobedience by Theo, who puts black and Filipino as his racial identity regardless of what the form he is filling out instructs:

> **Theo (abm 33)** – I don't really think about it. I just go ahead and mark Black and Asian even though it says mark one. Every application I fill out, I just mark Black and Asian and don't think about it. I just did it. Even if it says choose one, I choose two because that is what I am.

The claiming of both parents' racial backgrounds is one of the main components of the multiracial project, because for the large majority of United States' history we have used the "one drop rule" to determine a multiracial black person's racial identity (Nakashima 1992; Davis 1991). This historical understanding of racial categories puts extreme social, political and legal pressure on a person to claim one racial background, most notably the non-white racial category (Mezey 2003; Snipp 2003). Therefore, because twenty-two people in my study claim a multiracial identity, this suggests how strong the multiracial project has become in recent years. However, the reliance on biology to tell a person "what they are" is problematic to the process of assimilation, which tries to equalize and blend social differences (Hwang, Saenz and Aguirre 1997), because if biology is what we "are," is it possible to "blend" that away?

The Essentials of Race

The keys to using racial logic to figure out a person's race are grounded in essentialist notions of what specific races are supposed to look like, and what *should* be carried over when multiracial people are created. The most common identifying characteristics are skin color, eye shape, height, hair, noses, lips and overall body shape (Hall and Turner 2001; Root 2001). These essentialist notions of race would explain the recognizable pattern of people frequently placing multiracial people into mono-racial categories. Although the person asking the question may have picked up on certain physical or mental characteristics, most of the essentialist ideas of race were emphasized and (re)enforced as the multiracial person constructed an internal racial identity.

On looking Asian

When socially constructing the physical appearance of Asians, having almond-shaped eyes, yellow skin tones, straight black hair and petite builds were universally understood as Asian characteristics. Mandy states that her body type is the primary reason why people ask her about her heritage:

> **Mandy (awf 19)** – When I meet people, most people, the first time meeting someone they say, what are you? Or are you part Asian? A lot of times people know and they will say, you are half Chinese, because they are half Chinese. I think it's my hair and my body type because I am petite. It is just the way I look. My eyes and skin tone.

Mary uncovers that, although she believes that most people see her as white, when she dyed her hair black that allowed more people to see her Japanese background more clearly:

> **Mary (awf 23)** – Like when I tan, my skin is more yellow and my eyes are more Japanese to me, my mom, but it's not very prominent. I have some features, my hair isn't one of them, but when I dyed my hair black people can see it.

Jane drives home the point that straight hair is an Asian characteristic, because people will identify her as different races based on whether she straightened her hair that day:

> **Jane (abf 24)** – It depends on how I do my hair (laughs) … However, there is this wonderful invention called the flat iron, (laughs) and so if I have an hour of time then I will flat iron my hair. It actually comes out really nice. I have really long hair; it comes down to the middle of my back. If I flat iron my hair, I will have people coming up to me speaking Filipino, Spanish or other languages depending on whether they can see the fuzz or not.

After eyes, skin color, straight black hair and being petite, some interesting ethnic variations manifest themselves. Esssentialist notions of Asian people as petite become crystal clear if a person of multiracial heritage is *not* "petite." Although I did not interview people who were of Pacific Islander heritage, Josh and John found that people most often guessed that they were of this particular heritage because of their large size:

> **Josh (awm[4] 18)** – People mostly categorized me as Pacific Islander because I am large. When you are large people naturally say he is Pacific Islander like Samoan or anything like that because they have the same color skin and they are just bigger.

> **John (abm 33)** – Like let's say a fine young lady comes up to me and asked me my nationality. I will go ahead and tell them that I'm black and Filipino, because I do have features that a lot of people will mistake as Samoan. (laughs) So I have to let them know what I am.

While an essential characteristic for Filipinos is a flat nose:

> **Theo (abm 33)** – I got the Filipino flat nose. My mom used to tell me I have the Filipino nose.
>
> **Lenny (awm 22)** – Well my dad, he is a big white dude and has a big nose, so I have his nose. Not a Filipino mashed nose.

However, the question that I pose in this space is whether any racial characteristics are uniquely of a specific race? Do other groups have almond-shaped eyes? Do other groups of people have petite bodies or straight black hair? If so, then what does it mean for us to insist that one group of people has a monopoly on such body characteristics?

Although most of the people that I interviewed would agree to these essentialist traits, James begins to question the idea that Asians have a particular skin tone when he notices that many Asians, African-Americans, Hispanics and whites have similar complexions:

> **James (awm 22)** – My skin color should be perceived as Asian, but there are Hispanics the same color, African Americans that are the same color, they are real light. There are white people that have the same color …

This observation supports why biology, anthropology and sociology have disposed of biological classifications of race and situated this concept within the realm of social construction (Parker and Song 2001; Root 1996; Spickard 1992).

On looking white
Interestingly enough, after lighter skin color, whiteness was usually described in comparison to being Asian, rather than as a stand-alone essentialized racial category. Mary does this by comparing her hair color and height to what would be considered Asian:

> **Mary (awf 23)** – Here I don't think they really see me as Japanese at all. They say, oh, you have a Japanese mom, but with the culture it is very much appearance. In America, they say all Asians look the same, but I'm 5'8" and don't have black hair, and

so I don't think I'm identified as Japanese ... I look much more like my dad. I just have darker hair, and he isn't that much taller than I am, like 5'11". I have a shorter torso and Asians have a longer torso and longer legs. I think I look more white.

However, what Mary does not seem to mention is that there are white people that have black hair and that not all white people are as tall as her. By not stating white within clear physical terms suggests that she understands and acknowledges the diversity within whiteness, but not within being Asian.

On looking black
Skin color and hair texture were the most prominent physical features used to identify black people (Hall and Turner 2001; Root 2001). Although Theo thought that he looked like his mother and his father, he acknowledges how his skin tone and afro definitely locate his race as black for himself and other people:

> **Theo (abm 33)** – The afro is from being Black. I've got the tone I have a little bit of my mom's eyes. I have my dad's tone, I have exactly my dad's tone. I have both of their characteristics. My dad is the Black many would tell me the afro and my dad's tone, from my mom I had her eyes and nose. Pretty much when I look in the mirror I see black, I see black and Filipino, I see both my mom and dad. My skin tone was just like my dad's, my dad was black, but he has my tone.

A characteristic that was used to categorize being black for women were their figures, namely the size and shape of their hips. Sumi suggests that her hips are bigger than usual because of her black heritage.

> **Sumi (abf 20)** – My hips are bigger than usual and so is my butt. And my thighs are. My facial features aren't so Asian. I look at my brother's picture, and he is darker-skinned than I am, but he has more Asian facial features. That's how I can tell I look Black.

But what does "bigger than usual" mean? Who is she comparing herself to, Japanese women or just women in general? So, does this mean that *any* woman with big hips is of black heritage?

Although Reiko gives "credit" for her hips to her black heritage, she makes a connection between her mother's figure and her figure that deserves deeper analysis:

> **Reiko (abf 20)** – When I tell people I'm half black they say I don't look it, but they comment on my figure. (laughs) So I have to give my credit to something ... Well, I don't want to say black, but most women who are minorities are curvy people, and if you look at Japanese women they are very thin. Well, they can be curvy, but not as curvy as African-American people, and my mom is a very curvy woman and I have her curves. (laughs).

What if Reiko's mother was white and had big hips, would someone like Reiko suggest that her hips come from being black or that they come from her mother? Upon closer examination, the pattern that comes to the surface is that when multiracial people look like one parent or the other, they *assume* that those particular characteristics are essential to their parent's race, rather than just regular genetic variability. Although Fine et al. (2006) state that race is not an adequate means to address human variation, Reiko's comments reveal how much she depends on the concept of race to explain her individual variations.

The Influences of Phenotype on Internal Racial Identity

Regarding the development of an internal racial identity, Harris and Sim (2002) state that, "Although these identities need not be identical, they are not independent of each other" (Harris and Sim 2002, p. 615). The interdependence of internal and external racial identities became evident in the racial identification of Mandy, who identified herself as multiracial because she believes she looks multiracial to herself and to others, even though she identified culturally with being white:

> **Mandy (awf 19)** – I always say I am half Chinese. I really do characterize myself as being more White ... But I tell people Asian because they can tell I'm mixed with something, but I think of myself as pretty much white.

This strongly suggests that Mandy would not identify as multiracial at all if her phenotype did not "give her away." This statement is further substantiated by Ron who believes that he looks white to other people, and therefore, chooses to state that he is white in order to keep things simple:

> **Ron (awm 33)** – I usually don't, but more often I go with White. When I have the chance, I might say, I don't usually say Asian-American because I take that for Asians who were born in the United States. I don't have a good classification for myself unless

they give me mixed, White and Asian. Then I'll go with that. It
always seemed to be more complicated, so I usually pick White.

When asked why he did this, Ron believed it stemmed from his desire to not be different than the other white children he was growing up with at the time:

Ron (awm 33) – I think when I was younger, I didn't want to be so different. Especially where I grew up there weren't many Asians, and I think it was just generally easier to fit in and say White to make a lot of things less complicated. That would be my main motivation. Growing up here, I felt more White so it was easier, and I had less explaining to do.

Mary is viewed as just white, and yet has a strong Japanese cultural identity because she spent the first ten years of her life in Japan:

Mary (awf 23) – I define myself more Japanese just because I spent the first ten years of my life there. My mom pretty much raised me; my dad was on deployment most of the time, we were with my mom's side of the family. So from everything I know from right and wrong to how I do the dishes I learned in Japan. Therefore, I consider myself very Japanese ... I look much more like my dad ... I think I look more white.

Mary suggests that how white she looks is so overpowering that she only checks off white as her race because she does not look Japanese:

Mary (awf 23) – That comes a lot from I just don't look it, if I had any or more Asian traits I probably could identify myself with being more Asian, but it is very specifically Japanese in the way I identify myself. I don't feel comfortable putting Asian on there. It is easy for me to put Caucasian or white, whatever they put on there, one of the two.

The experiences of Mandy, Ron and Mary show how their internal racial identities were influenced by how they look to themselves and how they perceive they look to others. This data does not support Waters' (1990) assumption that racial differences would limit their internal racial identities to the non-white racial group. Interestingly enough, the experiences of Mandy and Ron suggest that for them, being of Chinese or Japanese heritage operated essentially the same as a symbolic ethnicity. Lived experiences such as these heavily support the idea that the assimilation process allows people of Asian/white heritage to construct an internal and/or external racial identity that converges with Anglo conformity.

Although the people of Asian/black heritage in my sample simplified their racial heritage, they were much less likely to simplify themselves down to a single racial category. Tyrone talked about simplifying his racial heritage from black, Native American, Filipino and Chinese to just black and Filipino:

> **Tyrone (abm 28)** – Usually when people ask what I am, I say Black and Filipino. My mom is actually Filipino and Chinese; her mom was Filipino and her dad was Chinese. My dad is Black and Cherokee Indian. I don't throw all that extra stuff in there though. So when people ask, I say Black and Filipino.

Aiko also simplified her racial heritage to just black and Japanese after asking her relatives and receiving a complicated web of possible races with no apparent certainty:

> **Aiko (abf 35)** – But we talked to relatives and found that my grandmother was part white and how that got there was my great-grandmother was raped by a master. And that was like, oh my God, because we're the product of slave masters right in our bloodline. Then we asked who our grandfather was, and my grandmother is pretty out there, and she said he was Puerto Rican from New York, but everyone else said he was Negro. So Grandma is black, but then I find that she is black, white and Cherokee Indian. So I thought, am I ever going to get a straight answer, but there really wasn't a demand on me knowing because race isn't a big deal to me. But as I've gotten older, I have wondered what it is.

Although people of Asian/black heritage seemed to be as willing to simplify their racial identity as people of Asian/white heritage, Lamont was the only person of Asian/black heritage that stated his racial identity as black, but he did so because he believed that other people largely viewed him as black:

> **Lamont (abm 29)** – Socially, I'm black, I'm African-American. But to be honest, sometimes I feel like we are a people all of our own. But yeah, I'm black ... Just outwardly, if anyone here looked at me I'm technically black ... Most Caucasian people look at me as a black guy.

However, Lamont makes a very interesting observation regarding how he thinks others see him. He states that in his personal experiences black people, unlike all other racial groups, normally can identify that he is not full black:

> **Lamont (abm 29)** – Black people wouldn't see me as just Black, they know something else is there ... Black people look at my hair and bone structure. They know who is full Black and who is not for the most part. That's what I've experienced.

These two quotes together deserve more analysis as to the reason why he states that he is "technically black." Lamont is connecting his internal racial identity to how he looks, but is also connecting it to what Caucasian people think rather than black people. Therefore, Lamont is acknowledging that his personal experiences have led him to understand that it is the opinion of what white people think his race is that is a driving force in his internal racial identity.

How Margaret identified herself racially presents a possibility of a melting pot identity. When asked what her race was, Margaret stated:

> **Margaret (abf 46)** – Just a person, a human being, I do not identify myself as anything but human. If someone asked me my nationality I will tell them, but I just see myself as the human. I don't split myself off into any other category ... Because I'm just like everyone else, I just happen to have a unique makeup but I'm just like everybody else. I'm not different than anybody else, no matter if they are Hispanic, white, black or Japanese. I do not consider myself a race, I'm just a person.

Margaret takes what Hollinger (1995) calls a post-ethnic approach to her racial identity. Hollinger states that a post-ethnic perspective remains alert to differences in ethnicities, but does not use the rigidity that is found with racial constructs. Margaret demonstrates this perspective by acknowledging her race when others ask her directly, but makes an effort to remove her internal identity from any racial constraints.

These experiences substantiate the claim that Davis (1991) makes that approximately 70 percent of African Americans are multiracial, and gives further evidence of how the "one drop rule" works. Tyrone's father is black and Native American, but he simplifies it to black. Aiko's father could be any combination of black, Hispanic, white and Native American, but she simplifies her father's heritage as black. Lamont's heritage is black, Native American and Filipino, but he simplifies it to black. This clearly demonstrates the continued social importance of identifying and being identified as black in our society. Therefore, unlike people of Asian/white backgrounds, the people of Asian/black backgrounds in my sample did not move towards a racial identity consistent with Anglo conformity, but in the case of Margaret, there is some evidence that there could be a movement towards a melting pot model of racial identity.

Most People Think I Look ...

Although many would acknowledge that multiracial people may have an ambiguous racial phenotype (Fulbeck 2006; Williams-Leon and Nakashima 2001; Gaskins 1999; Root 1996; Root 1992), most researchers and writers regarding this topic do not acknowledge, and therefore, do not address the fact that numerous people of multiracial heritage look like a completely *different* race than what they are mixed with. And if this is the case, then what does that mean for the vast majority of people that hold phenotype as the main determinant of race? In other words, is it possible to have an external racial identity that is not consistent with your racial background? And if not, why not?

... Latino

One of the most interesting findings that happened in my research was the preponderance of people of Asian/white and Asian/black backgrounds being phenotypically identified as a race outside of their understood racial backgrounds. The most common phenotype to be identified was "Hispanic" in general, but "Mexican" specifically in Southern California[5]. Although being identified as Hispanic happened to James, who is of Japanese, Korean and white heritage, and Patty, who is Japanese and white:

> **James (awm 22)** – If I go down to the swap meet, or if I go to an area that is predominately Hispanic, people will pick up or perceive I might be Hispanic or mixed with something, of course. But still seeing me as my skin colors, or whatever traits, they see me as being Hispanic.
>
> **Patty (awf 35)** – I just have had lots of people come up to me and ask if I am Hispanic. Hispanic is a big one.

All people of Filipino and white heritage in my sample had the experience of being identified as Hispanic, or more specifically Mexican:

> **Josh (awm 18)** – I look whitish; I can be mistaken for Hispanic instead of Filipino because I am not the typical Filipino guy.
>
> **Lenny (awm 20)** – I don't think I look White at all, everyone thinks I look Mexican.
>
> **Rudy (awm 21)** – But they never guess it, that I am Filipino or even part Filipino. So they always guess like Mexican, Mexican is a big one ...
>
> **Francine (awf 21)** – At parties, they ask what I am because my friends are White, so I pretty much stand out in Encinitas, and they will ask me, do you like tacos? Then I tell them I'm Filipino, and they say "no wonder why you're tan." That's all they say though.

Even though it was unusual, it was even possible for a person of Asian/black heritage to be identified as Mexican:

> **David (abm 37)** – Some thought that I was Mexican or Puerto Rican ... When I was in boot camp that was the first time I had my hair cut that short in my life, so a lot of people thought I was Mexican in those circumstances ...

However, being identified as Hispanic mainly happened to Asian/black people on the East Coast:

> **Lamont (abm 29)** – I found on the coasts, like the East and West Coast because there is so much diversity in California and New York ... I spend most of my time in California, but when I go to New York or Florida they guess me as Puerto Rican.
>
> **Cornelius (abm 35)** – When I was in New York, I lived in New York for four years; everybody thought I was Puerto Rican or Dominican.

Although he was identified as Puerto Rican or Dominican on the East Coast, when asked if he has ever been identified as Mexican, Cornelius states:

> **Cornelius (abm 35)** – No, because Mexicans look different from Puerto Ricans and Dominicans. There are dark and light-skinned Cubans too. I don't think I resemble Mexicans at all.

Although the people in my sample could have just believed that they looked Mexican to others, all have received verbal confirmation that they looked Mexican because people spontaneously spoke to them in Spanish or believed that they needed something translated into Spanish for them:

> **Patty (awf 35)** – I've had people come up and ask me if I speak Spanish to interpret something. Some people just come up and start speaking Spanish to me.
>
> **Rudy (awm 21)** – Oh, definitely when people think I am Mexican. Right when people try to talk to me in Spanish, I will be like, oh I am sorry, and then I am learning Spanish so I will try to talk to them. They will say something like gracias, and I will say something like dinero.
>
> **Cornelius (abm 35)** – Everywhere I went people started talking to me in Spanish, and I said, man, I don't know Spanish. (laughs) And they would say like, what happened, did your mother not teach you? And I would say I am not Spanish period. (laughs).
>
> **Francine (awf 21)** – I just feel discriminated against; sometimes they ask if I need something in Spanish all the time … when I go to gas stations and have to put in a pin number. They say they can translate it if you don't understand it.

This even happened with white people testing their Spanish on them, as experienced by Lenny:

> **Lenny (awm 20)** – I think they see me, they talk to me in Spanish, and all the white people when I walk into a store they think I am Spanish they say, you know White people. They think they know their Spanish and they will say "Como esta?" And I will say I am sorry, I am not Spanish. Everyone thinks I am Spanish.

Even though most situations relating to the misidentification of a multiracial person's race were normally cleared up in the beginning of an encounter or relationship, sometimes, like in the case of Leonard, the multiracial person found out that people thought they were Latino only after they told them their racial background:

Leonard (awm 35) – So, more often than not, I will get comments afterwards, if they find out what my race is, or what my ethnicity is, or how I identify, I will get comments like, oh, I thought you were Mexican. Oh, I thought you were Latino. And so, that is why I think most people assume that I am Mexican or Latino.

... Pacific Islander

Pacific Islander was another common phenotype that was used to categorize the multiracial people in my study:

David (abm 37) – Most people think I am Polynesian.

Patty (awf 35) – A lot of people ask me if I'm Hawaiian or Samoan ...

Timothy (abm 41) – People have mistaken my identity to be Hispanic, Hawaiian, Samoan, Filipino. I never denied it because I never had anything against it.

Karen (awf 18) – When people see me, the first thing they say to me is that I look Samoan or Hawaii.

John (abm 33) – A lot of Samoans that I went to school with would automatically think I was Samoan.

Josh (awm 18) – A lot of people thought I was Samoan for a while, it just came out with my friends in joking around because people did not really know. People would ask are you Samoan because I got called Samoan, Hispanic, Filipino, everything under the sun.

Although this identification happened to a lot of people in my sample, most people that this happened to classified themselves as "bigger":

Tomoko (awf 20) – I don't get it that often now that I've cut my hair and put on a little bit of weight. I used to be really tan and used to surf, so I think that is why.

John (abm 33) – Well, I'm a pretty large-framed guy, my color is tan. People just think that I have this Hawaiian look because I'm mixed.

Karen (awf 18) – With my body, not too many Asian girls are curvy. When I met with my family in Japan, my aunts were not really thrilled with meeting me, first, because I am a halfbreed, and secondly, because I am not the petite Japanese girl.

Josh (awm 18) – People mostly categorized me as Pacific Islander because I am large, when you are large people naturally say he is Pacific Islander like Samoan or anything like that because they have the same color skin and they are just bigger.

And just like in the case of being identified as Latino, language was often a mechanism to try and confirm their racial backgrounds, especially amongst women who seemed interested in the multiracial person in question:

David (abm 37) – Probably nothing, most people think that I am Polynesian of some sort. I have Samoans coming up to me speaking Samoan, and I am like, I am a black man. (laughs) Then they would say they were sorry and then start speaking to me in English. I am not even playing with you. When I bounce in some clubs and they have a Samoan crowd, the Samoan girls be talking to me in Samoan, and I am like, damn, shortie, I don't know what you are talking about, so speak English.

John (abm 33) – I could be walking through the mall, and I understand their language a little bit and I know they're trying to talk to me. And they will say, "What's up, 'uso'?", which means "brother" in their language. I still acknowledge those guys, but I know exactly what they mean. That lets me know that they think I'm Samoan. And with the Samoans that I do hang out with, for some reason the women become really attracted to me. (laughs) I don't know if that had anything to do with the question. So I must be a unique-looking Samoan dude.

So Why Not Join the Group You Look Like?

Although it was definitely possible to be accepted into a racial group that was considered different than one's heritage group, allowing themselves to be racially identified as anything other than their actual heritage was actively resisted on many different levels.

On one level, some people of multiracial backgrounds that were openly accepted by racial groups other than the races that they were comprised of would take on some of the culture of these groups, as in the case of Karen and Timothy:

> **Karen (awf 18)** – I think it's just appearances. When I did Polynesian dance, it was really easy to fit in, and if you put me up next to a Samoan or a Hawaiian girl I would fit that profile. A lot of other hapas do that because it's easier to take the role.
>
> **Timothy (abm 41)** – People have mistaken my identity to be Hispanic, Hawaiian, Samoan, Filipino. I never denied it because I never had anything against it. I have a lot of Hawaiian and Filipino friends, and I always considered myself a part of that but never the same race. Even in the white families, that's why I'm a cowboy fan, because I had friends from Texas. So I learned to adapt to different types of races like that. I got to sit in on their household, learn their culture and eat their food, and they would come to my house and get the same thing.

John was another that was very open to people's interpretations of himself as Samoan, but he was not willing to incorporate certain Samoan cultural elements, namely the lava lava, a cloth wrap that normally has a floral design that both males and females tie around their waists that resembles a skirt/dress:

> **John (abm 33)** – Sometimes I would have friends that knew I was black and Filipino and they would tease me and say I was Samoan. (laughs) When I was in the Army I had a couple of drill sergeants say, "look at this Junior Seau looking fool." I put two and two together after so many times of people thinking that I'm Samoan because of my complexion, but I'm not going to be out there wearing a lava lava. (laughs).

So, even though it was acceptable to associate with and take on cultural elements of different racial groups that one looked like, it was not acceptable for those same people to develop a racial identity based solely on phenotype. With Karen, her internal multiracial identity is a source of pride:

> **Karen (awf 18)** – I do like that culture and everything, but I am very proud that I am half Japanese and half White. Those two beautiful races put together made me, and I am very proud of that fact.

However, the essence of not identifying with racial groups that they were not direct descendents of came from a concept of *knowing* who you are:

> **Timothy (abm 41)** – No, I have always said I'm black and Japanese because that's what I knew.
>
> **John (abm 33)** – It doesn't really bother me that I look like some other ethnicity. As long as I know who I am deep inside it doesn't matter.

Although the idea that you can know who you are is directly linked to essentialist notions of what society claims race to be, it is key to note that *knowing* who you are racially for multiracial people extends past biology. In the case of Tyrone, although he knows that his mother is Filipino and Chinese and that his father is black and Cherokee Indian, he reduces his race down to black and Filipino because he feels like he does not *know* anything about them:

> **Tyrone (abm 28)** – I grew up mainly with the Black and Filipino sides. I don't know anything about the Chinese side or the Cherokee Indian side.

To further complicate the idea of knowing who you are racially, Josh, who *knows* very little about the Philippines and Filipino culture, claims an expressed Asian racial identity because of the desire to be different:

> **Josh (awm 18)** – I don't know any Filipino holidays or other special things. The only thing I could do is point where the Philippines is on the atlas and that's about all I got. I don't know the different subsections of the island and everything like that. I didn't even know what the Filipino flag was until just recently, so it's always like something I want to have. I want my children to have that Filipino race because it is just the diversity I love. I love knowing I am not like everyone else, even though we are all similar in skin color and everything like that and similar in biological structure, I just like knowing this makes me just a little bit different from someone else, even the Filipino population that is ever growing.

So *knowing* in this context is clearly not identified with knowing a culture. However, Leonard would suggest that knowing your race, and by extension, developing a racial identity, is a political statement in and of itself:

> **Leonard (awm 33)** – I mean like, somebody might claim that they are part Native American, but that doesn't run their life. You know, if it doesn't run their life, then I don't really care about that. If it is a significant factor in your day-to-day life choices and

neighborhood and personal discourse, you know, then go ahead and claim you're Native American, or claim you're Asian ethnicity. But if it is something that is just, like, cute to you, then I don't think you should claim it, politically.

Leonard takes this idea even further by suggesting that race is a metaphor for power:

Leonard (awm 33) – What I think the United States should be looking for, in terms of race, is how race is this manifestation of a metaphor for power.

Using race in this manner then makes the disassociation for Lenny and Gerald from Hispanic more understandable because of the social consequences of being identified as Mexican in Southern California:

Lenny (awm 20) – Absolutely, with me and my friends from San Diego they are all like Cambodian, and we were going to Vegas, and you know how you get up to the border they are like get down, "get down!", you know what I mean? I will say, shut up, dude, I'm not Mexican. It is funny, but I don't mind when my friends do it, it does not get to me. But sometimes when other people mistake me for it, it is kind of like I am not Mexican. It irritates me sometimes.

Gerald (awm 23) – They would say, why don't you go back to your country? It identifies me as being a minority, like I am not part of that group.

Therefore, although the people of diverse racial backgrounds in my sample do use essentialist notions of what race is and what race they are, this does not extend to thinking of race as just phenotype. In this section, one of the main factors that influence the construction of an internal racial identity is understanding how this identity fits into our current racial hierarchy and the consequences associated with that identity.

A Symbolic Pan-Ethnic Asian Identity?

Although people of Asian/white and Asian/black backgrounds do not readily identify as races that they phenotypically resemble, there are distinct moments were they take on a pan-ethnic Asian identity. This was normally done by claiming Asian cultural customs/traits that fell outside of the cultural characteristics of their actual Asian ethnicity.

James demonstrated a pan-ethnic Asian identity around his food preferences. Even though he was of Japanese/Korean and white heritage, he claimed food like chicken adobo (Filipino) and Panda Express (Chinese American) as his own:

> **James (awm 22)** – When I used to stay at my grandparents' some of the times, or me and my girlfriend and her mom is Asian and she is Asian and whatever, and we stay over there, like there was always rice, there was always chicken like adobo … We will eat at Hanna's, or a Korean style food place, Panda Express, any oriental type food.

For Brad, being of Chinese and white backgrounds did not stop him from driving a Toyota (Japanese) or practicing Tae Kwon Do (Korean) and Ninjitsu (Japanese and Chinese) in order to be more "Asian":

> **Brad (awm 20)** – Started off with Tae Kwan Do but did not like how they moved. Then I tried some Kung Fu but was too attention deficit for it, so I did not make it very far. Then me and my friend study Ninjitsu together … At the same time we bring in our rice rockets, I drive a Ford Focus, which is the closest thing that Americans make that you can rice rocket out. My previous car was a Toyota but I totaled it. (laughs).

While for Josh, trying to live up to the code of bushido (Japanese) is connected to him being Asian, even though he is of Filipino and white backgrounds:

> **Josh (awm 18)** – Personally identify? Before it would have been really low, but lately through my mind I have been going through a new Asian renaissance. I more take the characteristics not of Filipino but as Japanese … I try to stand up to the code of Bushido.

The women in my sample did not create a pan-ethnic Asian identity. Although there is no clear reason why this would not happen, this may have something to do with women being considered the carriers of culture in most societies (Williams-Leon and Nakashima 2001; Root 1996).

So even though there is some evidence that some people of multiracial Asian backgrounds create a pan-ethnic Asian identity, this does not function as a coalition building instrument in the manner that Yen Espiritu would suggest in *Asian American Panethnicity* (1992).

This analysis would actually more strongly suggest that Asian could become a symbolic race, rather than a symbolic ethnicity (Waters 1990).

Strategic Race: Seeing Internal Racial Identity as Strategic

The use of strategic race contradicts the notion that multiracial people are drawing closer to an Anglo or melting pot type of racial identity. Although Waters (1990) suggests that race would have more of an effect on the lives of people of multiracial backgrounds, there were distinct cases where a person's Asian background specifically took on a symbolic quality, but with precise strategic purposes. Strategic race differs from symbolic ethnicity in two significant ways. First, symbolic ethnicity uses ethnic heritage to justify certain symbolic acts of ethnic heritage, while strategic race uses biology to make claims into specific spaces, but does not necessarily carry with it any cultural behaviors of that race. Second, people that use their ethnicity in a symbolic manner do so without a presumed fear of social consequences, while the people who assert their race strategically do so because of the social consequences that they *expect* to happen as a result of their assertions and/or omissions.[6]

The strategic use of race and racial identity becomes even clearer in the cases of Jane, Richard, Josh, Lenny and Mary who identified their races in openly calculated and premeditated ways. Although Jane identifies herself as multiracial, she has claimed a Japanese identity in order to apply for a scholarship:

> **Jane (abf 24)** – In a specific instance, I put down my Japanese heritage because I was applying for a scholarship and you had to be at least one-eighth Japanese in order to receive it. So I knew I was half Japanese, and I actually did get the scholarship which was nice. It was for a Japanese women's club.

Richard remembers discussing which race he should identify himself as with the people around him, and they suggested that he claim his Filipino heritage so that he would be considered a minority on his college applications:

> **Richard (awm 31)** – My mother is Filipino. If I was to go percentage wise, I am Filipino. My dad is American Indian. As I was growing up in Ramona, people would tell me to check the Filipino box on applications because that would make me a minority.

However, further discussion with his college counselor suggested that he should select Native American even though he is only one-fourth Native American:

> **Richard (awm 31)** – Going to college being Filipino is not really a minority, especially in this area; when I saw the check box for American Indian, I would talk to counselors and they would say select that. Now when they ask what I am, I put down those two ... I was talking to a counselor, and from my understanding, at UCSD there are more Filipinos in the area and not so many Native Americans. I asked which one would be a better chance for me to get in, and he said Native American would be better.

Although Richard is not lying about his racial heritage, it seems that he adjusts his expressed racial identity for purely strategic purposes because he states that he has no cultural connection to his Filipino and Native American heritages:

> **Richard (awm 31)** – I don't understand their culture; I wasn't raised in that environment. I don't have any Filipino friends who aren't what I call "Americanized." I don't go to the parties, don't speak the language. The one thing that I would agree that I am Filipino is when I put the checkmarks in the boxes for applications because that is what I call myself ... If I chose what category to be into, I would say I am more Filipino than American Indian. I only put American Indian down so I could get into college.

Josh had a similar conversation with his mother regarding his expressed racial identity and the topic of college:

> **Josh (awm 18)** – The only time it's come up was when I started college; she said that I would need to use Filipino in order to get grants and things like that. And I understood that, especially going to a four-year college. It's going to help, at least hopefully.

This is another example of stating one's racial heritage for strategic purposes because of a lack of personal identification with being Filipino, but coupled with the realization that white people do not receive grants:

> **Josh (awm 18)** – I see myself as White. I still consider myself Asian so I can always have that leeway, that I will always have mark ... try to get a grant. Let's face it. White people do not get grants.

Interestingly enough, Josh also states that he uses his Asian background purposefully so that he can tell off-color jokes:

> **Josh (awm 18)** – I always find the politically correct forms of racial jokes not funny at all. Being Asian is a little easier, because if a white person is making a joke you can take it a little more severely. But if it's an Asian it's fine.

With further inquiry, Josh makes it clear that his claiming of an expressed Asian identity is based on the notion that people of color cannot be racist. This understanding was uncovered as Josh was describing how a black person called him racist while conversing on the internet. Rather than say that his comments were misunderstood as racist, Josh immediately states that this was a funny situation because the black guy did not know he was calling an Asian racist:

> **Josh (awm 18)** – Actually, online when I play video games all my different usernames are like "honky-tonk," because I am a big fan of honky-tonk. I play video games all the time. It is much funnier as "honky-tonk," because most people get a kick out of it. Some people think it is funny because one time I got yelled at and called a bigot online, because when you are playing you can talk to people, I got called a bigot online from a black dude. He said he was black and his name was like "black attack," I kind of assumed he was black, too. He called me a bigot online not knowing I am a large Asian man, so that was kind of funny.

Leonard would disclose his background in order to gain entrée into Filipino organizations:

> **Leonard (awm 33)** – I went to Filipino organizations, you know, trying to join the club, or participate, and they are surprised when I say I am Filipino. You know what I mean? Oh you are? They will be glad when they find out, but their gladness and their openness, once they find out, leads me to believe that there would have been some kind of closed attitude toward me until, you know? Closed until they found out I was Filipino. You know, they weren't unfriendly, but when they knew I was Filipino I felt like I had more entrée. Like I could hang with them more so.

However, Leonard found that disclosing his Filipino/white heritage closed doors for him with Latinos because they would assume he was Latino:

> **Leonard (awm 33)** – When it is with the Mexicans who think I'm Latino, or other Latinos think I am Latino, and they find that I am Asian, then I feel kind of like they close off to me a little bit. Like they let me in earlier. Not, not, huge. Not like oh, we can't talk about that, but, you know, a little bit like oh! We thought you understood. Like we understood your code, we thought you understood our code. So, they like explain things to me differently, or whatever.

They would do this even though he was well versed in the politics of Latino communities:

> **Leonard (awm 33)** – But I have been around it, been around Latino culture so much, my boyfriend is Mexican, his mom lives with us. We had a Mexican babysitter when we were growing up; my mom and dad speak Spanish. So, and we have lived in predominantly, I lived in predominantly Mexican neighborhoods for like the last five or six years. So, I pretty much feel in already.

Mary also used her expressed racial identification in a strategic manner when applying for a job. When asked if she has ever revealed her racial background on purpose, Mary stated that she has done so when she applied for jobs as a translator:

> **Mary (awf 23)** – I have a lot of the times to get jobs, but I don't know if it is on purpose. It helps because I work for the Vista School district to translate. It's whenever they need me to translate for a kid or for any parent-teacher conferences.

Mary was also encouraged by her mother to use her race in a strategic manner when applying for scholarships, and she states that she would consider this if the financial incentives become big enough:

> **Mary (awf 23)** – My mom has told me repeatedly you can get scholarships for being Japanese American, and we have scholarships at the center, so if I had more of an incentive I would go after them. When I go to a university, when I go to real school I probably will because it is so much money, but as far as community college goes you can pay for that. My parents have been very supportive with me and school, they help me out a lot.

John talked about how his brother used his race in a strategic manner when he was in prison. John stated that even though his brother looked more black than himself and was quick to state that his brother identified as completely black, John backtracked on this thought when he remembered that his brother identified as Asian when he was in prison:

> **John (abm 33)** – Yes, and now that I think about it he might identify with being Asian a little more than I thought. Because when you go to prison people hang out with each other, not by choice they tend to stick together in a racial context. Blacks stick with blacks, Mexicans with Mexicans and my brother when he goes into the penitentiary, he sticks with what they call the Asian car. That is what you call them. You have your black car, you have your Mexican car, it is who are you going to ride with, and you have your Asian car. So for my brother riding with Asians means to me that he somehow identifies with being Asian. And whether it is Filipino, Chinese or Japanese, those are the guys calling collect all the time, those are the people that he backs up. Although my brother has a long California curl, a jheri curl, (laughs), he looks more black than me. But if a riot were to happen then he would protect Asians first, because that is who he rides with.

When asked why his brother may have identified in such a manner, John was confident that his brother did so because Asians in prison were more likely not to get in trouble:

> **John (abm 33)** – But also he is with them because there is less trouble too. Asians usually kept their game pretty tight and they stay a lot more trouble free than the other cars, and my brother was not some high-powered, violent criminal. He stole a car, grand theft auto, and so he was in a different type of prison yard that did not require these real notorious people. And so anyways, there were a handful of Asians in there; Samoans, Japanese, Koreans, Filipinos were all in that one car. So he knew he was Filipino then even though he looks black. (laughs).

Although most of these examples demonstrate how racial differences can be capitalized on in situations where the risk is minimal and yet the benefits are potentially great, this tactic can backfire. While people can strategically use their race to give themselves certain advantages, Aiko represents a situation where the calculated use of her name to situate herself racially worked against her. When applying for a job at a Japanese restaurant, she felt that she received an interview because of her Japanese name, but things changed when they saw her:

> **Aiko (abf 35)** – I didn't get hired at a Japanese restaurant. The name was good but it didn't match the face. The name got me an

interview, but once I showed up they were stunned. So that didn't work out.

When asked how she knew that her race was an issue, Aiko explained that it was a combination of body language and what they said that helped her determine that:

> **Aiko (abf 35)** – It was the look they gave me when I walked through the door. Then they asked me if my name was Hawaiian, and I said no it's Japanese. My mom is Japanese and my father is black. Then their whole body language changed and they said that they were only interviewing people, but they weren't hiring. So it was obviously racial.

This suggests that strategically stating, or not stating, one's race does not work when the racial identity they are suggesting runs contrary to their actual phenotype in face-to-face situations. This option does not seem to work as well for people with Asian/black backgrounds as it does for Asian/white people.

Reflecting back on Jane, although she is of Asian/black backgrounds, when asked how the Japanese Women's Club confirmed her racial heritage, she simply stated that, "They knew my mom." This is an important distinction to make, because at the scholarship ceremony Jane made the social observation that all the award recipients were multiracial, but that they were all of Japanese and white backgrounds:

> **Jane (abf 24)** – It was kind of interesting, because there weren't any full Japanese children there. There were other recipients of different scholarships there and most of them were Japanese and white. I don't even remember another black and Japanese student there; they were all white and Japanese.

This begs the question as to whether Jane would have applied for the scholarship at all if the club did not know her mother in advance to her applying. Would she have felt comfortable claiming an expressed Japanese identity in an environment where they did not know her mother in advance?

Therefore, strategic race is a tool that is used to highlight racial differences for a conferred advantage. This is contradictory to the ultimate goal of assimilation, which is to blend racial groupings or to equalize their social positions.

Establishing Racial Hierarchy: Revisiting the "What are you?" Question

Separating ethnicity from race is an important distinction to make regarding race as a social construction, because ethnicity is changeable, while your race is not (Omi and Winant 1994). To tie such things as attitudes, aptitudes and abilities to a person's ethnicity is to suggest with time they will eventually become assimilated, while to connect these things to race is to suggest that they are fixed biological characteristics (Root 2001; Omi and Winant 1994). Believing that race is a biological fact, rather than a social construction is the essence to understanding how race is used to determine how people should be treated as a result of their classification within a racial hierarchy.

Understanding the "What are you?" question within the context of racial hierarchy allows for greater understanding as to why some people of multiracial backgrounds believe that the people who are asking these questions are not genuinely interested in them as a person, but only their race. In other words, people of multiracial heritage begin to feel like they are an "alien" or some type of zoo exhibit for people to observe, classify and categorize, but not have any sustained interaction with. This was how Reggie, an Asian/black male, felt after being asked about his race from a woman that did not even know his name:

> **Reggie (abm 22)** – Just randomly when meeting someone. I just met a girl the other day, and she's like what's your nationality? She's like, what are you? And I was like, dang, don't you wanna know my name first? It's funny how people want to know because sometimes they can't tell.
>
> **Interviewer** – Does that bother you?
>
> **Reggie (abm 22)** – If I don't know the person, sometimes I think, who are you? Usually it doesn't bother me; I'm a laid back guy.
>
> **Interviewer** – When people ask you, is it before they know your name or after?
>
> **Reggie (abm 22)** – It depends on the person. Usually girls ask me first thing, and guys ask me after getting to know me.
>
> **Interviewer** – And you've noticed this pattern?
>
> **Reggie (abm 22)** – Definitely.

Although curiosity could be the main factor, the fact that Reggie made a gendered connection may reveal that the women are trying to determine if it is socially acceptable to date him or not. Could he have "passed" for something else other than black, and these women were just making sure? What if they found out he was Puerto Rican or Cuban, would that have been more acceptable than being black?

Understanding the question within the socio-historical context of passing, the idea that someone of minority heritage could pass for white (Daniel 1992; Davis 1980) allows for a broader understanding of why people are so surprised to learn that Margaret's daughter has a Japanese and black mother:

> **Margaret (abf 46)** – They can't figure me out. At my daughter's school the subject comes up during class discussions and things like that, and my daughter is as white as can be. Everyone thinks she looks like Catherine Zeta-Jones. She has her own unique exotic look. And when the subject of race comes up, my daughter tells everyone that her mother is half black and half Japanese and they are amazed. And they will say, what? Oh my God, you're kidding me!

To be surprised is one thing, but to be surprised to the level implied by this quote is to suggest something else altogether. Although her daughter does not look black, by her own admission, now she will be regarded as black regardless of how she looks to her classmates.

Conclusion

In conclusion, the experiences of the multiracial people in my sample suggest that people of Asian/white backgrounds are experiencing a quantifiable level of assimilation, as they seem to be moving towards an Anglo conformity identity. The evidence also suggests that people of Asian/black backgrounds continue to use the "one drop rule" as a guide to constructing an internal racial identity, which I have argued is inconsistent with the assimilation process, because to maintain a racial identity is to maintain racial hierarchy (Zack 1993).

Also, through an analysis of the multiracial people in my sample, it was uncovered that the "What are you?" question is an effort by people to use racial logic to figure out the race of the people in my sample in order to figure out how they fit in the racial hierarchy. Both the Asian/white and Asian/black people in my sample expressed how others used essentialist racial notions to determine their race, which was key in placing them within society's racial hierarchy. In other words, to not know someone's race means that you do not know how to treat that person, because you do not know their social position.

Something else that was uncovered was that the multiracial project is at least partially responsible for broadening racial identity from the previous hypo-descent model to a model that encourages multiracial identification. Although this model allows people to "choose" their racial identity, it is clear that it does not challenge biological notions of race, rather it relies on them.

Also, the multiracial project has created what I call strategic race: the stating, or withholding, of one's racial background for specific beneficial gains. This space goes against common understandings of how people of multiracial backgrounds are supposed to be moving towards a homogenous racial identification. The strategic use of one's racial background is most commonly used when applying for scholarships, college and even for jobs. But strategic race also can be used to allow for a person of multiracial backgrounds to make off-color jokes and not appear racist. All of this, however, is tied to biological notions of race and deepens our connection to it, rather than shifting to a socially constructed understanding of race.

Notes

1. abf = Asian/black female
2. awf = Asian/white female
3. abm = Asian/black male
4. awm = Asian/white male
5. The connection between race and location will be further developed in Chapter 5, but here I will primarily focus on phenotypes.
6. Strategic race also differs from strategic essentialism in that it is used soley on a micro-level for personal gain, while strategic essentialism operates on the macro-level in order to establish groups.

3
External Racial Identity

The use of racial logic to construct racial categories is apparent when people of multiracial backgrounds quantify their assumed racial attributes, especially as it pertains to being Asian, while at times selecting a completely different identity than what might be expected from such a detailed list of specific attributes. This quantifying process began when the question was asked, "On a scale of one to five, with one being none and five being completely, how much do you identify with being Asian/white/black?" Asian racial attributes were quantified most often, but an interesting paradox emerged regarding how "Asian" someone identified themselves to be and how culturally Asian that person thought of themselves as being.

When I imagined the possible responses to the identification question, I thought that someone who spoke the language, knew the customs and practiced the culture would say that they were a five on this scale question, but this was not the case. Oftentimes, people who were born in their parent's foreign country came away with an Asian identity that was far less than I expected. This had much to do with the person's experiences and how that person was perceived racially in their foreign parent's native country.

On Being Asian, White, Black, or Multiracial

Establishing a Japanese Context

How people in Japan treated people of Japanese/white and Japanese/black backgrounds is largely due to two main factors: the belief that the Japanese represent a pure race, and the linking of multiracial children to their defeat by the U.S. in World War II. The notion of racial purity ideologically started after the Yamato clan defeated all other contenders and forced them into slavery and servitude, thus making this bloodline dominant in the creation of a Japanese race (Smythe and Naitoh 1953). Although modern historians acknowledge the multiple ethnic groups that originated Japanese people, this did not deter the Japanese from creating a racial ideology that was based upon its presumed purity:

> Many studies of Japanese society suggest the existence of a long-standing and almost unquestioned Japanese belief in myths of racial homogeneity and purity: "Ideas about the racial purity of the Japanese have little scientific or historical credibility, but two centuries of self-imposed isolation from the seventeenth century fomented myths about common bloodlines." These myths are seen as having been reinforced by prewar and wartime nationalism. (Morris-Suzuki 1998)

Immediately before and during WWII, this racial purity was imbued with a racial essence which stated what the Japanese were:

> In general these consisted of a strong sense of loyalty and super-patriotism, tremendous assimilative power which enable Japanese to adopt the best of a foreign culture and yet remain distinctly Japanese. Further, they were told they are especially endowed with superior powers of organization and unmatched ability for expansion and achievement ... All of these were supplemented by frankness, kind heartedness, optimism, an affinity for purity and cleanliness, propriety and order, and a soft and patient disposition. (Smythe 1953)

These twin constructions led to a boom in scientific racism and allowed many researchers to develop anti-miscegenation stances that made their way into public discourse:

> Although he recognized that the Japanese people themselves were the product of earlier phases of racial intermixture, Koyama took a negative view of colonial intermarriage. In strictly biological terms, he believed that intermarriage could produce either benign or malign results, depending both on social circumstances and on the nature of the "blood lines" that were mixed in the process. (Morris-Suzuki 1998)

The relationship that the United States has with Japan did not create the negative attitudes towards interracial relationships and multiracial children, but it did facilitate making children of Asian/white and

Asian/black backgrounds symbolic of Japan's defeat in WWII. People of multiracial heritage faced huge problems in post-war Japan for a number of reasons:

> Their problems of being racially different in a race-conscious society are compounded by other modal features of their lives: illegitimacy and father-absence, culturally presumed immorality on part of mother, and the lower social class status of mother. (Burkhardt 1983)

The precarious social position of their mothers led to many multiracial people experiencing rejection by their mothers and humiliation by childhood peers (Ibid.). Although many multiracial children were a product of illegitimate means, many children would have been spared some of these experiences if the United States had not actively refused to allow interracial families to go with the father back to America, which had to do largely with the fact that anti-miscegenation laws were not deemed unconstitutional until 1967 (Wadlington 2003; Burkhardt 1983).

Therefore, establishing a pre-war WWII anti-miscegenation ideology is important to understanding how the lived lives of people of Japanese/white and Japanese/black backgrounds are affected by their interactions with Japanese people; however, this situation was exacerbated by Japan's defeat by the United States and the creation of multiracial children that ensued afterwards. It is with this context in mind that we examine the lives of two women who were born and raised in Japan.

Mary and Ai
Mary and Ai were born and raised for a large portion of their lives in Japan, yet their identities were moderated by how people treated them based upon their external racial identities. After living in Japan for the first ten years of her life, Mary stated that she had only a moderate Japanese identity, or a three on a one-to-five scale. I felt this was an interesting response because of how Japanese she believes she acts:

> **Mary (awf 23)** – My mannerisms and the way I think are Japanese ... I still to this day don't use the dishwasher my entire life, cause even to this day my grandmother does not have a dishwasher, most people in Japan don't ... Anything from that small to I go over to my friend's house, the first thing I do is take off my shoes, when I get home the first thing I do is take off my shoes. It's just the way I do things, everything I do is related in the way I was raised, and I was very much raised Japanese.

Although Mary has a strong internal Japanese racial identity, she states that Japanese culture does not do well when someone is different, which is consistent with previously stated literature (Morris-Suzuki 1998; Burkhardt 1983; Smythe and Naitoh 1953). To illustrate this point, she speaks about the time she was going to a Japanese private school and had to get her hair cut because it was not as straight as the rest of the Japanese girls:

> **Mary (awf 23)** – The school that I went to, we all had to have the same haircut, and Japanese hair is much more coarse, heavier and very straight and mine had little flips here and there, so I had really long hair when I first started and they told me I had to cut it. They had five people to hold me down to cut my hair, and my nuns were serious because I had a little flip in the back, and you had to have straight hair and I had a little accent of hair. They never had to encounter something different like that, I think I kind of threw them into shock.

This difference in how she looked was even noted and affirmed by her mother who stated that Mary is different on the outside, but is Japanese on the inside:

> **Mary (awf 23)** – Yes, I knew I was different. I don't know how much it affected me because my mom always told me you don't look anything like these girls but inside you are just the same. I really was, I grew up the same as they did.

Mary's phenotype not only affects how people view her, but also affects how people treat the actual abilities she possesses. This difference was noted regarding her ability to speak fluent Japanese. Mary states that Japanese people have a very standoffish attitude with her language abilities because she does not look like she should be able to speak Japanese as well as she does:

> **Mary (awf 23)** – Yes, it is like they have their boundaries broken. It is different if they first meet me, I've ever seen them before and they learn that I speak Japanese, they are still uncomfortable with it. I think the idea of talking the way they do with other Japanese people and with someone who doesn't look Japanese is kind of uncomfortable.

Mary goes even deeper and states that she lived in a paradoxical state for the first half of her life because in Japan she looked different, but acted the same, while in the United States she looked the same, but acted different:

> **Mary (awf 23)** – Over there I was different because I looked different and it was very superficial. Here I was different because I looked the same and acted different, it was something much deeper and that I think was harder to get over than just being perceived as different because I looked different.

The effects of an external racial identity can overwhelm someone's internal racial identity, which was the case with Ai. Born and raised in Japan for the first nineteen years of her life, when asked the question of how much she identified with being Japanese, Ai stated, "Not at all." When asked to explain why she felt this way, she states that it is because people saw her as different, and therefore, did not accept her, even though she was a girl who acted just like them:

> **Ai (abf 57)** – I was just a girl. I wore a kimono just like everyone else, but I just couldn't go a lot of places. They didn't accept me. They would call me names, and I would feel uncomfortable. They would look at me because I'm different and point their finger at me. So I think my mother believed that I should just stay home.

It is obvious that after living in Japan for nineteen years that one would have the cultural qualities of being Japanese, however, Ai makes it clear that *being* Japanese is more important than *acting* Japanese:

> **Ai (abf 57)** – You have to be straight Japanese. So no matter what you did, sports or anything, I was not good enough for them.

In other words, it was more important to *look* Japanese than it was to *act* Japanese (King 2001).

Establishing a Filipino Context

People of Filipino/white and Filipino/black backgrounds have a decidedly different experience in being multiracial, due in part to centuries of colonialism which led to the creation of a mestizo class in the Philippines (Hernandez-Chung 1975). Little to no research has been done on a pre-existing racial state for the Philippines, however, race relations in this region were heavily influenced by 381 years of Spanish, United States and Japanese colonialism (Larkin 1982).

The Spanish, centered in Manila, intermarried with Filipinos, creating a mestizo class that was wealthy and heavily identified with European ways (Hernandez-Chung 1975). Also during Spanish rule, many people of Chinese heritage, which served as a middleman minority, also established a base of mercantile operations in the Philippines and intermarried with the native population (Larkin 1982). The population of Chinese mestizos became a large and discernable population by the 1740s, and still dominates retail, wholesale and import trade and many of the cottage industries:

> The mestizos, blending the economic skills of their Chinese fathers and the native culture of their Filipina mothers, penetrated farthest into the interior, often serving as agents for merchants of the larger settlements. (Larkin 1982)

Although Filipinos have more history regarding people of multiracial heritage, this by no means suggests that all multiracial people were treated equally. Although Spanish colonial rule may have indirectly set up white privilege, the United States colonial period directly established white supremacy regarding how Filipinos were thought of and how they were treated. Initially, Filipinos were equated to a black person, which was used as justification for the United States to colonize them because of the prevailing ideology that people of color could not govern themselves (Ngozi-Brown 1997). However, Filipinos were given an intermediate status within the racial hierarchy when justification was sought to give the Philippines its independence (Tyner 1999).

The establishment of white privilege allows us to make some sense of how Tyrone developed his internal racial identity. Born and raised for the first five years of his life in the Philippines, Tyrone stated that he identified as only moderately Asian, or a three on the one-to-five scale. This was interesting because of how strongly he identified with Filipino culture and his ability to live in the Philippines with no problem:

> **Tyrone (abm 28)** – I would say about a three. I was mostly raised with the Filipino way. I understand and can speak Tagalong and I cook Filipino food. My mom taught me how to cook Filipino food. I was raised on the Filipino side ... I speak the language. I know how to cook Filipino food. Pretty much I could live in the Philippines and not have any problems.

However, Tyrone's internal racial identity is moderated by how he looks and how people treat him because of it. Tyrone makes it clear that:

> **Tyrone (abm 28)** – I think of myself half Filipino and half Black. I don't consider myself more one race versus another.

And when asked how closely he identified with being black, he stated that he was moderately black, a three on the one-to-five scale. However, when describing why he identifies as being black, it immediately becomes an issue of how he looks rather than his cultural upbringing:

> **Tyrone (abm 28)** – The way I talk and there is no way around my skin color. (laughs) I can't fake that ... People judge me based on the color of my skin. Like I said, a lot of people can tell I'm mixed, but some people are ignorant and bigots and want to judge me based on skin.

Therefore, as we can see in the experiences of Tyrone, it seems that in order to be Filipino you have to look Filipino, not necessarily act Filipino. As was the case with Mary and Ai, Tyrone's experience in the Philippines and in the United States was dominated by racial essentialism.

Constructing Race Through Physical Location

Research conducted by Landale and Oropesa (2002) on the Puerto Rican population has produced results that strongly connect the physical location of a person to the racial identity they develop. The authors demonstrate how Puerto Ricans on the mainland are much more likely to identify as Hispanic or Latina, while on the island they are far more likely to identify as white, black or triguena (a mulatto classification). Many multiracial people observed that people used racial logic to identify their race by connecting it to their actual physical location (Hall and Turner 2001; Mass 1992; Williams 1992). James suggests that his external racial identification can be affected by which basketball court he decides to go to or what area he decides to shop in:

> **James (awm 22)** – I would play at Washington Park in Escondido; I haven't played over there in about a year or a year and a half. But when I was going there, that predominately Hispanic and African American, white boys don't go down there. Spanish people would come up and start talking to me in Spanish, and they look surprised when I say I don't speak

> Spanish. If I ask if they speak English, they will look very surprised and say they don't know. I don't know but they just assume. Maybe because it is where I am because that could have something to do with it.

People at the basketball court are using racial logic to connect James to the area, and since the area he plays basketball has a predominately Hispanic population, people readily interpret him as being Hispanic.

Some people, like Lamont, suggest that their racial identification is affected by whether they are on the East or the West Coast. They state that they have been considered Hispanic on the East Coast, but not on the West Coast:

> **Lamont (abm 29)** – I found on the coasts, like the East and West Coast because there is so much diversity in California and New York. Most of the stuff in between is what are you. I spend most of my time in California; when I go to New York or Florida, they guess me as Puerto Rican.

Location also affected whether people spoke Spanish to Cornelius who states that he has never had anyone speak Spanish to him on the West Coast, but has had people regularly speak Spanish to him on the East Coast:

> **Cornelius (abm 35)** – People mistake me for everything. They know I'm mixed with Black, but out here they think I'm Samoan or Islander. When I was in New York, I lived in New York for four years, everybody thought I was Puerto Rican or Dominican. Everywhere I went people started talking to me in Spanish, and I said, man I don't know Spanish. (laughs) And they would say like, what happened, did your mother not teach you? And I would say, I ain't Spanish period. (laughs).

Therefore, to be interpreted as Hispanic on the East Coast allows darker-skinned people to be considered Hispanic because of the wider variety of looks within this racial grouping in that part of the country. However, on the West Coast, the Hispanic population is generally assumed to not be as dark, therefore, directly affecting the lived lives of multiracial people.

The country that you are in can also affect how people racially identify a person of multiracial background. For Ai, her racial identification dramatically changed in every country she visited:

> Ai (abf 57) – Other times when I went to the commissary, some Marines would speak to me in Spanish ... When I went to Brazil, they spoke to me in Brazilian, but I didn't understand that. (laughs) Also, when I went to Mexico, they spoke to me in Spanish there.

Although it is possible that people spoke to Ai in Spanish when she was in Mexico because that is all she spoke, it is also possible that in Mexico the locals understand and accept the fact that there is a wide variety regarding who could be Mexican when one is in Mexico.

The experiences of James, Lamont, Cornelius and Ai suggest that the concept of race itself is spatially located, and suggests that racial logic is being used in this space to connect a person's race to their physical location and might be applied on a local, national and global level. However, this conclusion seems contrary to Landale and Oropesa's (2002) statement that Puerto Ricans who lived in Puerto Rico *resisted* using the racial definitions of the United States. My sample suggests that racial categories are specific to specific areas, so Puerto Ricans are not *resisting* racial categorization, but rather, they are using the available racial categories of the place they find themselves.

Constructing Race Through Language

Language is also at the disposal of racial logic and is used to locate people racially (Hall and Turner 2001; Hall 1992), with the most common language used in my sample being Spanish. Spanish speakers would often approach a person of multiracial background assuming they were part of a Spanish speaking ethnicity, which was the experience of both Rudy and Patty:

> Rudy (awm 21) – Oh, definitely, when people think I am Mexican. Right when people try to talk to me in Spanish, I will be like, oh I am sorry, and then I am learning Spanish so I will try to talk to them. They will say something like gracias, and I will say something like dinero.

> Patty (awf 35) – I just have had lots of people come up to me and ask if I am Hispanic. Hispanic is a big one. I've had people come up and ask me if I speak Spanish to interpret something. Some people just come up and start speaking Spanish to me.

Or non-Spanish speakers would try and accommodate a multiracial person who they thought was Hispanic:

> **Lenny (awm 22)** – I think they see me, they talk to me in Spanish, and all the white people when I walk into a store, they think I am Spanish they say, you know White people. They think they know their Spanish and they will say, "Como esta?" and I will say, I am sorry, I am not Spanish. Everyone thinks I am Spanish.

Therefore, not only do people of Hispanic backgrounds assume that Lenny's external racial identity is Hispanic, but also so do white people. However, he would not have been able to assess what they thought of his heritage if it were not for moments like this when white people made their assumptions clear regarding his external racial identity. This begs the question as to whether people "treat" Lenny like he is Hispanic, and if so, what are the social consequences of this treatment?

Japanese and Filipino languages were used to locate people racially also, but they operated in the reverse where Japanese and Filipino people would speak their language around multiracial people, not knowing that they understood perfectly what they were saying. Mary observed this behavior frequently while talking to Japanese people because she believes that they think she is white, while Tyrone actually overhears Filipinos talking about him in an ethnic store:

> **Mary (awf 23)** – The fact that I would put it forward and try to speak Japanese with them, but they will always come back to me in English, and it is like the mannerism they give me ... They just become much more timid like they know they can't talk shit around me (laughs) ... it is like they have their boundaries broken.

> **Tyrone (abm 28)** – We pick up Filipino food, and I can hear people speaking Tagalong, and normally they would say, what's he doing here, laughing saying he don't know what to do with that. When I was younger, I had a bad mouth, I used to say stuff back to them, but being I have respect for my mom I don't say anything now. We go and pay for things, I speak Tagalong and people are shocked.

Also, with Ai the presence of an accent made people seriously reconsider her external racial identity, while for Sabrina, the lack of an accent made people less likely to accept her internal racial identity:

> **Ai (abf 57)** – The thing they notice is my accent, and so they asked me what my nationality is, and I tell them I'm Japanese and black. That's what I tell people. I rather say that than say I'm just

black, because I don't know what I am, but I know I'm mixed. (laughs) That's how I categorize myself all the time. I always tell everyone that I'm a Japanese mix.

Sabrina (awf 49) – I think it is because of the way I talk. In their minds if I am from Okinawa, I shouldn't talk as clear. They don't realize that even though my mother is from Okinawa, I went to primarily American schools. In their mind they think I talk well compared to a lot of other Asians. They don't see the other side of the mix.

Margaret, because of her seemingly completely ambiguous racial identity, actually gets questioned by both Asians and Hispanic people:

Margaret (abf 46) – Asian people will stop me and ask if I'm Filipino. They will pick an Asian nationality. They're the ones that are really bold and stop me wherever I am and ask me usually if I'm their race. So that makes me feel that Asian people see some Asian in me. Hispanic people think I'm Hispanic because they always talk to me in Spanish. (laughs).

Although this seems innocent enough, Margaret describes a situation with a Hispanic man that suggests that her not speaking Spanish is because she is ashamed of her presumed Hispanic heritage:

Margaret (abf 46) – One time I went to 7-11 and a Hispanic man was behind the counter and he starts talking to me in Spanish. I said, excuse me, but I don't speak Spanish. Then he looked at me really weird and said it is not right to look down on your heritage or something like that. (laughs) I was shocked, and my mouth just flew open, like what? He said it's not right to deny your heritage, you know. So a lot of Spanish-speaking people speak to me a lot in Spanish if they see me somewhere. So that's why I think they see me as Hispanic.

The consequences of not speaking Spanish are far more serious for Aiko's son, who was beat up because he did not speak Spanish:

Aiko (abf 35) – Most people think my children are Hispanic. As a matter of fact, my son was jumped once in a bathroom by six Mexicans because he wouldn't speak Spanish back to them, and they said, do you think you're too good to speak Spanish? He tried to tell them that he's black and Japanese, but I guess they didn't believe him.

Although these situations make people of multiracial backgrounds feel unwelcome and unaccepted, what is clear from each of these experiences is how the ability to speak a language is racialized. Why would someone white not be able to speak Japanese? Why would someone black not be able to speak Tagalong? Why could a black person not have an accent? Or why must a person who is part Okinawan speak with an accent? This all suggests that we use race as a type of shorthand to assess a person's abilities, aptitudes and attitudes, but when people do not fit into any pre-existing racial common sense, then racial logic becomes mandatory in order to resolve seemingly disconnected racial clues.

Cultural Attributes Versus Racial Stereotypes

Although cultural attributes of a particular ethnic group are often construed as racial stereotypes, the need to distinguish between these two concepts is necessary for this study because the multiracial people in my sample use both cultural attributes and racial stereotypes to construct their internal, external and expressed racial identities. Culture is "an organized body of conventional understandings, manifest in act and artifact, which, persisting through tradition, characterizes a human group," (Ogburn 1937, p. 161) which suggests that cultural attributes are specific quantifiable conditions that would arise from such a context. While racial stereotypes, unlike cultural attributes, are, "attitudes composed bodily and uncritically without any basis in experience or knowledge" (LaViolette and Silvert 1951).

Simply put, cultural attributes benefit from a specific cultural context, while racial stereotypes are inherently fallible because of the assumed biological basis for such attitudes, abilities and aptitudes, and are designed to fix that racial group's social position in our racial hierarchy (Virtanen and Huddy 1998). Putting this difference in action, it could be said that a cultural attribute of Japanese people is respect for their elders due to the emphasis of the Buddhist religion in their culture, while a racial stereotype would be to say that all Asians are submissive. The first is an attribute that can be directly linked to Japanese cultural emphasis and can change over time, while the second is a stereotype that is linked to essentialized notions of race, which makes the connection seemingly permanent and biologically driven. It is between these two spaces that the people of Asian/white and Asian/black backgrounds of my sample construct their racial identities.

Fitting the Stereotype

The convoluted nature of racial identity is displayed in this section as the multiracial people in my sample struggle with their internal and expressed racial identities, as they use racial logic to navigate through racial stereotypes and cultural attributes. Social understandings of race, I argue, serve to "push" and/or "pull" people of multiracial heritage towards a particular racial identity. "Push" and "pull" factors are usually associated with reasons why people migrate from country to country (Takaki 1989; Reimers 1985), but actually serve as a useful framework for understanding the internal racial identity development of multiracial people. Not fitting socially constructed appearances, attitudes, aptitudes and abilities serves to "push" a multiracial person away from a particular identity, while fitting into these understandings "pulls" them towards a particular identity.

On fitting Asian stereotypes

Most, if not all, Asian stereotypes fit into a model minority framework of Asians being thrifty, smart and hardworking (Kim and Lee 2001; Smythe 1953). Being smart in general, but strong mathematical ability specifically, pulled people to at least partially identify with being Asian, because it was always described as deriving from that person's Asian heritage. This was not only true for the multiracial person, but Ai noticed that other people's racial logic brought these stereotypes together as well:

> **Ai (abf 57)** – A Japanese girl that I used to work with said that I was smart because I was Japanese. But they don't know who I am, so I try to tell them so that they don't have to guess. I want them to know who I am, because it's taken a long time for me to accept myself.

However, not being mathematically inclined served to push Mandy away from identifying as Asian:

> **Mandy (awf 19)** – People would assume that I'm really smart, in class people would say, "ask Mandy for help," and I would say I don't know how to do it. (laughs) Or people will say that I did really well on my SATs. They would just assume it ... Chinese have a stereotype of being really smart. But my mom says this is not true; they just work harder. (laughs).

Another attribute of Asians was their work ethic. Although Patty acknowledged that both of her parents are hardworking, she still relies on race to explain her work ethic:

> **Patty (awf 35)** – I have said that because I'm Japanese. I think it is because my mom said I was a hard worker. I mean, look at me; I'm a single mom with two children, and I have two jobs. I'm just a hard worker. I don't know if it is because I'm Japanese. I just have two hardworking parents who don't want to see me fail. My mom is Japanese, and Japanese are very hardworking people.

Patty even takes a distinctly cultural activity, origami and using chopsticks, and equates it to her racial heritage:

> **Patty (awf 35)** – My creativity, arts and crafts and working with my hands I would say that it's on my Japanese side. I like to do origami which you have to have hand and eye coordination. Working with the chopsticks is very well for hand-eye coordination.

James represents a person who has an internal Asian identity partially because his father is of Korean and Japanese heritage. However, James mostly associates his internal Asian identity with his lack of desire of being associated with the stereotypes of being white on the basketball court. By understanding how people use race as social placement, James understands that being identified as white on a basketball court will suggest a plethora of various negative stereotypes:

> **James (awm 22)** – I don't like been associated with white because of all the negative connotations of being a white boy, because I play basketball ... You are not as skilled or gifted physically, can't jump high, can't run faster, can't dribble the ball, so you know Asians tend to be a little more athletic, not that they tend to be, they are a little more coordinated because they are not all tall and gangly, or the common misconceptions that white people can't jump high, they are not fast.

When asked what about being Asian would make someone think that he was good at basketball, James stated that Asians represent an unknown quantity, and therefore, are thought of as better than white because whites are a known quantity:

> **James (awm 22)** – You can't be labeled as a white boy playing basketball, you know, otherwise you will be like my brother,

slow, can't play defense, just a shooter, good free throw shooter, can't play a lick of dee, no quicks, definitely no ups. For me it was like even on our own basketball team, good friends going to school for 6-7 years ask how come I can jump and my brother can't? And they'll say, because I am Asian. See, for Asians, it is not like African Americans or European players. Asians are the unknown.

Therefore, because the concept of race is supposed to give people insight and knowledge of a person's abilities, being good at basketball when you are of Asian/white backgrounds *must* come from being Asian because it is *known* that white people are not all that good.

Being tight with money is another Asian stereotype and is the only thing that Mandy associates with being Asian:

> **Mandy (awf 19)** – Also, I think that Asians are a lot more frugal or cheap, and I wouldn't say I'm cheap, because I go shopping and spend a lot of money. But at the same time, I do actually think about the better deal. I do consider those things, but that may actually be because of my dad who is pretty frugal too. But a big part of my mom's family is that they are all really cheap. (laughs) They all have this mentality like we're living in the Depression. I don't know if this comes from them living in China or they feel like they have to hoard everything, but I feel that way. Not to their extent, but I do consider it.

Although stereotypical in nature, Mandy may have developed this context as a result of her parents meeting in New York. Research suggests that the Chinese in New York tend to have an overall lower socio-economic status than their California counterparts who tend to be more educated, and their Hawaiian counterparts who tend to be more economically successful (Boyd 1971). Therefore, because of their lower status in New York, this may have caused her Chinese relatives to be a little bit tighter with their money.

Therefore, people of Asian heritage are socially constructed as smart, mathematically inclined, hardworking and cheap. And since these attributes are tied to biology, it suggests that they are permanent and unchangeable.

On fitting white stereotypes
Although Asian was interpreted as giving people of multiracial backgrounds intelligence, a strong work ethic and the ability to tightly manage money, whiteness was constructed as multifaceted. James suggested that being white contributed to a laid back social demeanor:

> **James (awm 22)** – That can be another thing I can identify with being white. I'm more laid back; I don't have that drive to be the most intelligent. I might act that way in life but not with studies.

While Mandy also associates being social and well-balanced with being white, which pulls her towards a more white internal identity:

> **Mandy (awf 19)** – ... I wasn't like the other Chinese girls who were focused on their studies, and that wasn't me, I had a balance. I was really social. I just felt like since I'm not full Asian, I'm not going to bubble in Asian. So I just bubbled in white.

Patty believed that her musical talent was derived from her white side:

> **Patty (awf 35)** – My being a musician. I played the clarinet and the French horn. I would say it comes from the White side because my dad was a musician. I think I would say I associate it with the White side.

And Gerald, fascinatingly enough, felt that he was more masculine than his Filipino cousins because of his white heritage:

> **Gerald (awm 23)** – Because physically I am a lot taller. I have a lot of facial features from my father who is Italian. Filipinos' noses are flatter and I don't have those features. I have more masculinity. For example, some of my cousins are homosexual. They seem not to be strong physically.

So whiteness cannot be adequately generalized because in essence it is only what other races are not. Asians are driven, while whites are laid back; Asians are nerdy, while whites are social; Asians lack imagination, while whites are creative; Asians are feminine, while whites are masculine. In other words, Asian and black people are a particular way, while white people do not act or think in a particular way.

On fitting black stereotypes
Being athletic and being able to dance were normally interpreted as a result of a person's black heritage. Although Ai never thought of her running ability as coming from her black heritage, she makes it clear that other people used racial logic to make this connection:

> **Ai (abf 57)** – No, I never thought that because I'm black I do better. It's because I try hard. No one gave me anything, and so I

had to try hard to get things. But my Japanese classmates would say it's because I'm "kurumbo," because I'm black and so I'm good at sports. I don't know where they heard that from, but that's what they said.

In the case of Sumi, a 20-year-old Asian/black female, her friends and other acquaintances would sum up her abilities along racial lines, especially her dancing:

> **Sumi (abf 20)** – They mostly say it because if I were to do something that they thought was Black, they would say "oh that's the Black side of you." Like the way I dance, they always say that it's my Black side. If I was at my friend's house and we had dinner, I would usually help with the washing of the dishes. My friend would say that I didn't have to, and that what I was doing was my Japanese side. I think, well, do Black people not do this stuff?

This last statement is powerful because of how far it reaches into how racial logic constructs multiracial people. To say that intelligence comes from being Asian is to suggest that white and black people are not intelligent. To say that athleticism comes from being black is to suggest that white and Asian people are not athletic. Therefore, Sumi demonstrates a high level of critical thinking by challenging essentialist racial notions. Unfortunately, this is not the rule, but the exception.

In instances where a person of multiracial backgrounds fits key stereotypes, racial logic is used to bring these disparate stereotypes together in one racialized body. This is illustrated by Cornelius who identifies his mathematical abilities as coming from his Japanese heritage and his athleticism to his black heritage:

> **Cornelius (abm 35)** – Growing up I was fairly smart, I had the mathematical mind and a mechanical mind, because I'm a machinist, I program machines all day long. I could do it in my sleep, because it is all math and math always came easy to me, and I always said that was the Japanese side of me and the sports were my Black side. (laughs) I always looked at it that way.

Separating race from culture is an important distinction to make regarding race as a social construction, because to tie such things as attitudes, aptitudes and abilities to race is to suggest that they can never be adjusted, shifted or changed because they are biological in nature, not social. Believing this construct is the essence to understanding how race is used to justify how people are treated as a result of these racial classifications.

What About the food?

Another factor that played a role in racial identity formation was food. Liking the food of a particular race normally pulled a person closer to that race, while not liking the food served to push them away. Tyrone described his ability to make Filipino food as an advantage over other Filipino Americans:

> **Tyrone (abm 28)** – I know how to cook Filipino food. Pretty much I could live in the Philippines and not have any problems. A lot of American Filipinos here, if they were to move to the Philippines they would have problems. To me it seems I have an advantage over most Filipino-Americans growing up here now.

James, who has an internal Asian identity, describes how there was always rice when he would go to his Japanese grandparent's house, and that if he or his Asian father wanted any rice that they would have to make it themselves:

> **James (awm 22)** – I can identify because I love the food ... When I used to stay at my grandparents' some of the times, or me and my girlfriend and her mom is Asian and she is Asian and whatever, and we stay over there, like there was always rice, there was always chicken like adobo. Or teriyaki chicken and seaweed always that stuff was there, and my grandma's house the same thing. There was rice always cooking, walk in the door there is always rice. And when I go home even my dad will sit there and go if we ever want rice me and my dad would have to cook it.

James takes his expressed racial identification even further by stating that the "white people food" that his mother cooks is not appealing to him at all:

> **James (awm 22)** – ... I don't care for the food my mom cooks. She cooks stuff like Special K loaf, green beans and mashed potatoes like white people food. (laughs) I am just keeping it real, this is how it works in my house. We eat broccoli, we eat carrots. My mom thought seaweed was something you put in a plant to make it grow. Anything that is oriental in our refrigerator was my grandparents, or I would buy it from the Japanese market.

James even adds that his mother is a vegetarian, but does not separate this fact from his mother's whiteness regarding her choices in food preparation:

> **James (awm 22)** – She is vegetarian, but all the good stuff that's oriental is fish, beef, and chicken. She eats like fried rice or oriental noodles, but she would much rather have her Special K vegetarian loaves ... I can bring some for you because it is pretty special. (laughs) That you have to put ketchup, soy sauce, sour cream, anything to help it not taste like Special K loaf. Is that bad, to classify white people food? She will make veggie burgers and french fries, and spaghetti, and we have pancakes for dinner and I will say, whatever, Mom.

Francine and Josh, who both have an internal white identity, do admit to eating some of the mainstream Filipino dishes. However, Francine equated eating most Filipino food with an episode of *Fear Factor*, a TV show that regularly has contestants eat bugs and worms in order to win money, while Josh states that Filipino food is just nasty:

> **Francine (awf 21)** – They see me as Filipino and think I would eat that fish with vinegar. They ask me to eat with them and I'm thinking hell no. And as soon as I walk in I know my mom's friends are there because I can smell it. You have no idea, it's like fear factor. (laughs).

> **Josh (awm 18)** – They say, how could you not like fish? I would say, I never really had the taste for it and the same thing for other Filipino foods. Sometimes it grosses me out, you just have to stay maintained because you don't want to be insulting. Because whenever I would go to my other Filipino friend's for dinner, some of their food looks nasty, okay.

Theo describes his food preferences from both sides of his heritage as an expression of his racial identity:

> **Theo (abm 33)** – Most of the time if race is brought up, it is just by asking what nationality I am. They would say they are Filipino, and I would say my mom is Filipino too. We start talking foods and everything, that's how it always is ... Adobo, pansit, sinagong and lumpia, things like that. On the Black side it's greens, jambalaya, gumbo, crayfish, which is from my dad. (laughs).

He continues this discussion by stating that he even eats Filipino food that most other Filipino/black people don't like:

> **Theo (abm 33)** – Since you bring that up, there was a guy I worked with who was Filipino. One day he brought dinigowan which is pig meat. They cut it up and boil it in water and vinegar. After that they take pig's blood and pour it in there and boil it until it is a thick brown. A lot of Filipino/black people don't like that ... I opened it up, and Kareem said, oh, you like dinigowan? And I said, yeah, do you? And he said no. I don't know if that has anything to do with it. A lot of people don't like certain foods, but I was brought up on everything. The only Filipino food that I don't like is leu gow, that's the soupy rice with chicken in it. That's like kryptonite to me, man. (laughs).

When asked by this uncle which food Theo prefers to eat, he states that there is always room for both:

> **Theo (abm 33)** – Then my father's brother who lives in Bristol, he's like, do you eat jambalaya? He says, are you going to eat the soul food, or are you going to go over there and eat the Filipino food? And I go, there's always room for both. (laughs).

This effect seemed to be a little bit stronger for people of Filipino backgrounds, probably because Japanese and Chinese food has become mainstream in American culture in general, but especially in Southern California. By liking both foods, this allows Theo a justification for having such a strong internal multiracial identity.

Conclusion

Building on the theoretical framework of the last chapter, I have focused this chapter on how people of Asian/white and Asian/black backgrounds in my sample develop external and expressed racial identities. What was uncovered was that the respondent's race was spatially located on a local, regional and national level as they went from place to place, coast to coast and nation to nation. Race was also located by use of language in order to confirm racial group membership. Concerns for the assimilation process arose when the experiences of the multiracial people in my sample seem to suggest that racial understandings are something that people learn *through* the assimilation process, which strongly suggests that race is not something that can be ignored, negated or unlearned.

Lastly, how well one fit the cultural attributes and the racial stereotypes of a particular racial group played a central role in how the multiracial people in my sample chose to identify themselves. Fitting a particular attribute or stereotype served to *pull* a person towards that particular racial identity, while not fitting served to *push* them away. Again, these findings question the inevitable endpoint of the assimilation process, because stereotypes are used to place someone racially and are a product of our culture. Therefore, the assimilation process teaches people what race they are and where they are placed on our racial hierarchy, which strongly suggests that race is not something that a person can simply leave behind.

4
The External Context of Racial Identity Formation

It is a common understanding within both public and academic discourse surrounding people of multiracial heritage that multiracial people challenge racial categorization and will eventually bring the end to the usage of racial categories (Williams-Leon and Nagashima 2001; Root 1996; Zack 1993). However, three main assumptions must be drawn out to analyze the implied validity of these challenges: first, that the existence of people of multiracial heritage actually does challenge our current racial construction (Spencer 2011; Thornton 1996; Spickard 1992); second, that multiracial people do not internalize essentialist notions of racial categorization (Daniel 1992; Nash 1992); and lastly, that people of multiracial backgrounds somehow experience less racism than other people because of their ambiguous phenotypes (DaCosta 2006; Guevarra 2003; Streeter 1996).

Although these three assumptions exist in many separate spaces, all three of these assumptions are clearly illustrated by David A. Hollinger in his book, *Postethnic America*, where he states that people of multiracial heritage, especially those of Asian/white and Asian/black backgrounds, challenge how race is socially constructed in the United States. Hollinger argues that these two groups of people challenge present day racial classifications because they are without a distinct history of being relegated to any specific racial category, and because of the assumed inability of our current racial construction to absorb them. Therefore, Hollinger suggests that multiracial people will eventually invalidate the concept of what he calls the "ethno-racial pentagon" by continued assertions of their multiple ethnic identities.

Racial Effects on Attitude and Behavior Receptional Assimilation

Although compelling, by equating race to ethnicity Hollinger does not recognize how the concept of race affects the assimilation process. Therefore, this chapter will focus on how people of Asian/white and Asian/black backgrounds experience race in their everyday lives and to what level they are attitudinally (the absence of prejudice and stereotypes) and behaviorally (the absence of discrimination) assimilated.

In order to do this, I will analyze whether the racial identities of people of Asian/white and Asian/black backgrounds are the result of a "rational" or a "constraining" dynamic:

> Relative to Asian-white children, the racial identity of Asian-black and Asian-Hispanic children may be more constrained because of the overriding emphasis that society places on their being half-black or Hispanic. (Xie and Goyette 1997, p. 555)

This suggests that a "rational" racial identity would lead a person of Asian/black background to have more of an Asian identity because of the presumed advantages of not being identified as black, while a "constrained" identity would result in an identity that is less Asian because of the social pressures to identify as black. Although this is supposed to be used within an Asian/black framework, I also will apply the rational/constraining proposition to Asian/white people to see if their racial identities are affected by such a dynamic. However, for this group, the rational racial identity would be considered white, while the constrained racial identity would be Asian.

A Pro-White Context

One of the main tenets of racial formations is that racial categories change with time, and many people would argue that multiracial people are the impetus for our current reconstruction of racial categories (Lipsitz 1998; Omi and Winant 1994; Davis 1991). However, what racial hegemony would also dictate is that as things seem to change, the basic fundamental building blocks of race would stay the same and remain centered on white supremacy (Winant 2001; Omi and Winant 1994). Although people of Asian/white backgrounds do not have a history in the United States that extends as far back as people of Native American/white and black/white backgrounds, we will see in this chapter that the multiracial project is currently in the process of reconstructing, reinstituting and reinforcing white supremacy within the experiences of people of Asian/white heritage.

Anti-Asian racism
White supremacy was expressed in direct anti-Asian racism with Sabrina who spoke of the numerous times she had been referred to as "Jap" by both whites and blacks. However, Sabrina gave a detailed story regarding a big white boy who continuously called her "Chink":

> **Sabrina (awf 49)** – I think I was about in the ninth grade, and the boy was in the eighth grade. Everyday he would call me "Chink" and make me cry and feel bad. One day I got tired of crying, and I told him that we should settle this. We did, and I beat the crap out of him. After that he never bothered me again. This was a White boy who was big. I just got tired of it, and I took care of him.

Putting this story in its proper context suggests that this happened when she was about fourteen, which would have made the year about 1971. This timeline puts the U.S. in the middle of the Vietnam Conflict, which represents a time of high anti-Asian racism. However, what one must take special note of was the usage of "Chink" by this white child to describe someone of multiracial Japanese and white backgrounds. The broad manner by which anti-Asian actions, as illustrated in the case of Vincent Chin, have been used to describe all Asians and Asian Americans was the major impetus of what Yen Le Espiritu called pan-Asian ethnicity, where Asians of all ethnicities came together under socio-political distress and helped form our current conceptualization of Asians and Asian Americans today (Espiritu 1992).

Josh also experienced rejection, but this came from his grandfather who lived in Alabama:

> **Josh (awm 18)** – Yes, I've been rejected once because of that from my father's dad. I never met him in my entire life. I talked to him once on the phone at about four, and he said he didn't want to talk to me because I was a mixed blood. My dad grew up in Alabama. He never really accepted any of my dad's choices, my dad had a really bad childhood. So he doesn't really accept my dad that much, especially marrying a Filipino wife and having a different child.

Sabrina and Josh's experiences represent the lack of attitudinal and behavioral assimilation regarding Asians in general, but multiracial Asian children specifically. However, I would argue that this was more the result of the historical time frame and the age of the grandfather because no one else of Asian/white backgrounds in my sample reported experiencing any overt racism in their lives. This strongly suggests that people of Asian/white backgrounds are being assimilated into the American mainstream.

Pushing whiteness as a parent
White privilege was asserted by both Asian and white parents, as white parents demonstrate a constraining effect on their children's racial identity as they try to force whiteness upon their children. Rudy spoke of how his white father continuously tried to instill an internal and expressed white racial identity for his children:

> **Rudy (awm 21)** – Throughout my life I would go to either side, either White or Filipino. My dad would always try to make it White because we are living in a White world and your life is pretty much White. Then I got tired of going back and forth trying to be White. People would give me a hard time for trying to assume the White role even though there are obvious things about me that are not totally White. So I decided that I am neither of them. I am both; I am in my own category.

His father's assertion that this was a white world confirmed the fact that people who identified themselves as white have a distinct social advantage to the point where he is encouraging his son to "pass" for white, rather than assert his multiracial background (Daniel 1992; Davis 1991). Although not stated explicitly, many have argued that white parents who have tried to assert their white privilege through their multiracial children were the main reason for the beginning of the multiracial project in the first place (R. Spencer 2011; Parker and Song 2001; R. Spencer 1999; J.M. Spencer 1997).

Even though Rudy came to understand himself as his own category, this was not always the case, because he made it clear that he wrote on most forms that he was white:

> **Rudy (awm 21)** – It kind of stopped after high school when I told him. But ever since the beginning, whenever he would say, like when we would have to fill things out for paperwork, or like whatever, I would put White. My mom never told us to have Filipino pride ... Here is a good example, my mom wanted to teach us the Filipino language, and now we know that every kid's brain can absorb more when they are younger, so it is best to teach them when they're young. My mom wanted to teach us Filipino and my dad said no because that would confuse us.

This quote represents the struggle that Rudy has with his father and the creation of his own racial identity. Although he does check-off white as his race, it is obvious that Rudy and his Filipina mother wanted him to at least identify as being multiracial. However, it is equally as clear that Rudy and his other siblings speaking a foreign language in the U.S. would challenge the identity his father was trying to construct for them.

The assertion that children who learned two languages in the home often get confused may have seemed plausible and even reasonable for a concerned parent; however, white supremacy clearly raised its head within the school system, which placed Rudy in a class with speech-impaired children when he stated that his household spoke two languages:

> **Rudy (awm 21)** – I actually had to go to speech class when I first went to elementary school because when they ask what language I speak, my mom spoke Filipino, so when they asked me I said both. So they actually put me in speech class for people who had a speech impediment, and they were trying to get me not to practice Filipino ... They were telling us not to practice that, I felt very stupid in my class because people with speech impediments are people with speech problems.

When his father found out, he demonstrated his knowledge and understanding that this was a white world because he was upset at his son's admittance to speaking two languages in the household, rather than be upset that the school system treated his son in such a derogatory and demeaning manner:

> **Rudy (awm 21)** – I don't think I told anybody, and my dad was pissed that I was in there because he got mad and said, "Why did you tell them Filipino?" He said, "We all don't communicate that way. Your mom speaks it and you guys just overhear it sometimes when she is speaking it or talking to your aunt." I can imagine how that made him look.

What is intriguing regarding the quotes from Rudy is that although he identified himself as white on government forms, he struggled with his father's demands by asserting his multiracial heritage at key moments. So, what does it mean when a child willfully goes against his father's wishes regarding his racial identity? Perhaps it means that Rudy's racial identity was important enough to him to disobey his father over it. Or perhaps he was testing the grounds of what it will mean for him to assert his racial identity later in life.

The relationship that Rudy has with his father presents an interesting dynamic in regards to rational and constrained racial identities, because it seems like Rudy is fighting off what would be considered a rational identity choice in being identified as white, and advocating for the constrained racial identification of being multiracial. Whatever the case may be, it is obvious that Rudy's racial identity is important to him and he is willing to fight for it.

A constrained white racial identity?
The rational versus constrained racial identity framework seems to take another hit as people of Asian/white backgrounds who look very white, according to themselves and others, developed a constrained internal white racial identity. The person that best exemplified this construct was Mary who had spent the first ten years of her life in Japan, and initially had a strong internal Japanese identity:

> **Mary (awf 23)** – I define myself more Japanese just because I spent the first 10 years of my life there. My mom pretty much raised me; my dad was on deployment most of the time, we were with my mom's side of the family. So from everything I know from right and wrong to how I do the dishes I learned in Japan. Therefore, I consider myself very Japanese.

Although she internally identified as being Japanese and her immediate family accepted her, she always knew that others thought of her as "gaijin," an outsider:

> **Mary (awf 23)** – I think it helped going to the store daily and stuff because they knew they could approach me, it hurt when we went outside of the bubble to go on vacations. We would go to Tokyo or to my grandfather's hometown, which is smaller than my town and they've never seen a "gaijin," an outside person. I would get different reactions, it would be a little confusing, but I don't think I knew the extent to it.

The feeling of being an outsider is consistent with Japanese attitudes towards people of multiracial heritage (Williams 1992), and eventually affected Mary to the point where she no longer asserted her Japanese cultural traits to Japanese people because she knew they felt uncomfortable around her:

> **Mary (awf 23)** – I get a vibe that they are uncomfortable with speaking to me in Japanese ... I have taken Japanese classes and there are Japanese people in the class, and even then it takes them

a while to warm up to me to speak in Japanese, then halfway through the semester they realize I can hold a conversation. The fact that I would put it forward and try to speak Japanese with them, but they will always come back to me in English, and it is like the mannerism they give me ... They just become much more timid, like they know they can't talk shit around me. (laughs) And they're like, oh, did she hear anything we said? They can be sitting at the next table talking about someone; it doesn't have to be me, necessarily.

Ultimately, this negative treatment led Mary to develop a constrained white racial identity because she felt like she was not treated like she was Japanese by Japanese people and by others. In other words, it was "easier" just to be white:

Mary (awf 23) – Not in Japan, here you always have the standardized test, I put Caucasian just because it is easier ... I don't know who looks at them, and if they make that much of a difference because it has Asian on there I think, but I don't find myself being Asian, I find myself very much specifically being Japanese. That comes a lot from I just don't look it, if I had any or more Asian traits I probably could identify myself with being more Asian, but it is very specifically Japanese in the way I identify myself. I don't feel comfortable putting Asian on there. It is easy for me to put Caucasian or white, whatever they put on there, one of the two.

Although it was not a privilege to be treated in such a degrading manner by people of Japanese heritage, when the social context is changed from Japan to the U.S., the privilege that Mary and other people of Asian/white backgrounds experience lies within the ability to create a racial identity that *is* constrained, but that suffers few ill effects within an American context because of white privilege.

An Anti-Black Context

Although there was an overall disdain for all multiracial people, it is clear that people of Asian/black backgrounds were more often singled out and intentionally discriminated against in Japan (Morris-Suzuki 1998; Burkhardt 1983). Although Japanese understanding of themselves as racially pure (Smythe 1953) played a role in how they conceptualized black people, the important concept to set up in this section is the fact that an anti-black context is established through a worldwide perpetuation of white supremacy (King 2001; Valverde 2001; Winant

2001). To not understand or accept this notion would severely limit the scope of this analysis and its ability to explain how the people of Asian/black backgrounds in my sample experience racism from people of Asian and white heritage, but also from people of black heritage.

Anti-black racism from Asians
The establishment of racial hierarchy through the media played itself out in the lives of people of Asian/black backgrounds through racist encounters with other Asian people. Ai was born and raised in Japan and spent the first nineteen years of her life as a "kurombo," which is "nigger" in Japanese:

> **Ai (abf 57)** – Because when I was small no one accepted me for who I am. If I did well in school I was cheating. So when I had a friend, I told them an idea and they would steal it. I'm about to cry now. They would steal my idea, and then tell me they wouldn't want to play with me anymore because I'm "kurombo," which means "nigger." My whole life was like that.

This anti-black sentiment was persistent throughout her life and was also present in her own family, as Ai remembers not being able to develop a close relationship with her aunt because of her external black identity:

> **Ai (abf 57)** – My mother couldn't take me to a lot of places because of how people looked at me because I was different. My mother's cousin is well-off, but I can only visit them once a year because they don't accept me and they don't accept my mother. My mother's twin sister doesn't accept me either, and so she doesn't accept my mother. When I got older and got married, my mother's sister accepted me a little bit, but not much, because her son works a government job and it's embarrassing. So I never got to know my mother's sister.

One must also take into consideration that Ai is 57 years old, placing her birth only five years after WWII ended, which I am certain intensified her racial experiences. However, anti-black attitudes were also present with Tyrone with his Filipino family members, as he remembered how his aunt always sat his mother's family outside of her restaurant and always talked down to them:

> **Tyrone (abm 28)** – My mom's sister doesn't like that we are half Black. She has a problem with that … She just doesn't like Blacks … She owned a Filipino restaurant, we used to have to eat

outside, and she'd bring us the food. When we ate inside, my aunt would talk down on us, and my mom didn't want us to hear it.

When asked if the negative attitudes towards black people were shared by all Asians and not just his aunt, Tyrone quickly claimed that, "No, it's just her." However, this did not seem to be the case as Lamont explained the color hierarchy in the Philippines:

> **Lamont (abm 29)** – In the Filipino heritage in general, the lighter you are, the more respected and the wealthier you are. The darker Filipinos tend to live up the mountains and are poorer. I had a hard time when I got married because my wife is Filipino. Her father didn't even come to our wedding. Now that we have children, he is my best friend now. It was difficult for her family to accept me because I wasn't Filipino enough.

This quote strongly suggested that there was a pre-existing color line in the Philippines that was constructed during Spanish colonialism and reinforced through the U.S. and Japanese colonial period (Ngozi-Brown 1997; Larkin 1982). However, the idea that a pre-existing color line existed was also suggested by Aiko, because in Japanese culture dark skin was seen as dirty:

> **Aiko (abf 35)** – My sister asked my mom what that was all about, and my mom said they're not used to seeing our color because they don't like it. They think it's dirty, and that's how it is over there and that's how they are. That's when I understood why we couldn't be backstage, or we couldn't watch any of her shows because we were black and no one knew my mom's husband was black.

The association of people of Asian/black backgrounds to "dirty" strongly suggests that the experiences the Japanese had with the Eta and associating them to being "dirty" was a useful, if not necessary, precursor to categorizing black people in general, but Asian/black people specifically, as inferior (Donoghue 1957; Smythe and Naitoh 1953).

Aiko's experiences with anti-black racism by Japanese people also happened within the context of the United States. Aiko recalled an incident of how badly she and her sister were treated when they were hanging out with their mother while she was trying to give dance lessons to Japanese people:

> **Aiko (abf 35)** – Because being Japanese, Japanese people are very racist. My mother was a Japanese cultural dance teacher and it was at this time that I experienced racism from the other side. My mother traveled everywhere with this dance group, and one time my sister and I went with her. We usually never go with her because we were clingy, and she would push us away so she could do her stuff. As soon as she would see us, she would stop what she was doing and tell us to get out. When we were young I just thought I couldn't be in there, but now that I'm older I think her pushing us out had to do with them looking at her kids and seeing we were dark. So one time she was teaching in Gardenia, and we walk in with my mom and the record stops. (laughs) She told us to wait over in the corner and I was oblivious, but my sister figured it out quickly and told my mom that we were not going to wait there and that we will go driving around for a little bit. So we come back a few hours later, and when we knock on the door the person inside cracked the door open, and we said we're looking for our mom, and they said that we had the wrong place and slammed the door shut. We knock again and tell them our mother's name and they say oh, but then slammed the door shut again. Then my mom comes to the door and tells them we're her children. By this time, the whole house is at the front door. My mother goes to get her stuff in, the little girl comes up to us with the stereotypical bowl cut and pan face and says, why are you so dark, don't you wish your skin was peach like us? And my sister said no, because if we did, then we'd look like you. I thought it was a little harsh to say to a six-year-old, but my sister was pissed! (laughs).

Even though many could argue that the Japanese people in the house were just skeptical of strangers, as many people are, the depth of this incident only revealed itself to me when I considered if I would even treat a stranger in such a manner. This treatment strongly suggested that being black magnified being a stranger to the household residents.

Although Aiko's experience with anti-black racism could be partially ameliorated by the idea that she was perceived as a stranger, Jane experienced direct anti-black racism with her Vietnamese friend's parents, as she was told to wait outside because the parents did not want a "black" person in the house:

> **Jane (abf 24)** – I never had a problem with Filipinos, but it's kind of funny, growing up with Vietnamese friends, I've actually been kicked out of some homes because I'm black. I don't speak Vietnamese, but I've heard parents yelling at their kids, who is that? And then my friend would say, could you please wait outside, my mom doesn't like black people in the house. Another

friend's house that was also Vietnamese, they were hanging out when the parents were gone, and when they came home I asked, do I have to leave? Because I was conditioned that Vietnamese people don't like black people, and he said, no, it's okay, you don't look black today. So you can stay. And a year later I had lightened up, and I was allowed into the first person's house, the one I got kicked out of, and I thought to myself, maybe I don't look so black.

Such negative behavior from Asians of all ethnicities toward blackness did not create a constrained black identity as it did for some people of Asian/white backgrounds to create a constrained white identity. As a matter of fact, such open hostility toward people of Asian/black backgrounds from Asian people actually created a resolve in Cornelius and many others to claim a rational internal Asian and black identity no matter what Asian people thought or how they may treat them:

> **Cornelius (abm 35)** – I'm half black and half Japanese. I embrace both sides. My mom raised us with all the traditions and culture. My dad raised us; he was always there for us. In the big picture, I know Japanese have a negative opinion towards Americans period, and Blacks. Everybody has a negative opinion toward Blacks, but I identify with both.

However, I will argue in the next section that one of the main reasons why people of Asian/black backgrounds did not create and continuously fought against a constrained black identity was because of the anti-black racism of white people.

Anti-black racism from whites
It has been clearly documented that racism in the United States was based upon a white/black paradigm (Lipsitz 1998; Steinberg 1995; Marable 1995), and if you did not fit into either category, then you were placed somewhere in between (Davis 1991), as was noticed by Sabrina in her school environment:

> **Sabrina (awf 49)** – I will never forget this one time in second grade in South Carolina, I noticed that all the White children sat in the front of the class, and all the Black children sat in the back. I was brown so they didn't know where to put me. There weren't any brown people at the time in the South. It was either black or white. Most of the time I was in the middle.

However, the strongest manifestation of this system of thought was to place you as either white or non-white, which occurred in the life of Margaret who grew up in a segregated neighborhood:

> **Margaret (abf 46)** – Well, I grew up in an all-white neighborhood back in the 60s, and although people had rights, people did not treat you very nicely. Since I didn't fit in at the school and I didn't have blonde hair I stuck out like a sore thumb and I would be spit on, laughed at, you name it and it has happened to me. People beat me up, because I looked different ... They called me the n-word and stuff like that. People were chasing me and spitting on me, just the kids from school whose parents were obviously prejudiced and it rolled onto the children.

Even though Margaret had made it clear that she looked racially ambiguous enough to be placed in such disparate racial categories such as Filipino, Hawaiian, Samoan and Mexican, in the social context of the 1960s she was interpreted as non-white, which made her black by default.

Though people of Asian/black backgrounds fought against a constrained black identity, this did not stop white people from treating Asian/black people as if they were just black. Tyrone stated this notion clearest with his observation that when tensions run high, white people were quick to call him a nigger:

> **Tyrone (abm 28)** – People who have racial tensions are quick to call me nigger because of my skin color. One time we played San Pasqual, I played with this white guy, we are actually really good friends now, and him and I got into a fight on the football field because he called me a nigger. I don't know, somehow we became friends, and he still apologizes to me to this day. (laughs) People who are bigots are quick to call me nigger.

Being called a nigger by white people in the heat of the moment was a common theme with almost every person of Asian/black backgrounds that I interviewed. Theo explained that angry customers would call him nigger even when he was the main person trying to help them:

> **Theo (abm 33)** – A customer, my friend who was Mexican was helping him out. And sometimes it gets really busy, and sometimes you have to wait a while. But regardless of being fast or slow, we make sure the job is done right. For some reason he must have waited over an hour and a half, but he was told it would be thirty to forty-five minutes of a wait. He leaves, then he

comes back and it has been an hour and a half and we still haven't gotten to his car yet, and he left his cell and nobody had called him to let him know that it would be a little bit longer. So when he had talked to the sales person that had helped him originally, he started getting wild. And I said, "Now, sir, we can help you out," and the first thing he said was, "Get away from me, you fucking nigger!" And I was like, whoa, shit. And I go, "Sorry, but he will be right with you." I don't know what that word means, I just always knew from what my parents taught me and the movies and stuff that it was always a bad thing. So I was like, alright. So I went into the office and said, he's ignorant. It went in one ear and out the other.

Getting called a nigger happened on football fields, in stores and even at home, as Aiko spoke about an argument with her white boyfriend when they lived together in the Midwest:

> **Aiko (abf 35)** – Once I had a white fiancé who was in the military, and when he got out we moved to Indiana, and I didn't realize he drank a lot, and one day he got mad at me and called me a fucking nigger. He said, you are a fucking black bitch, a fucking nigger, and we were at my grandmother's house and he pushed me across the room and that was the last time I saw him. We were engaged for three years, lived together and had two kids together, and it seems like he was okay when we were in California because there's so many different races and I looked exotic when I was younger. But when we went to the Midwest, I think my dark skin just made me black. His family was okay, but his friends made comments like, you got some of that brown stuff, and that was too much pressure for him. He became more abusive, called me a fucking nigger and pushed me across the room, and that was that.

Although being called nigger in a highly emotional setting was how most racist incidents were experienced by people of Asian/black backgrounds, we must remember that racism can be cold and calculated when necessary. This deliberate assault on blackness was carried to the radio waves, as Lamont recalled having the former grand dragon of the Ku Klux Klan talk to him when he was on a radio show:

> **Lamont (abm 29)** – In a concert we did, after the show there was a burning cross. This was out in Fallbrook. We did a radio interview, and Tom Metzger, a leader in the KKK, called in. We tried to witness to him and asked him to come to one of our concerts. He said yeah, but only if we came out to one of his. And I thought to myself, oh no, because they do the skinhead thing. I

don't remember the radio show, but the topic was about how multiracial things could come together. It was pretty unique, because he used to live in Fallbrook and he's like the grand dragon wizard or something of the KKK ... He thought it was cute what we were doing. He wasn't ignorant, he sounded intellectual. He didn't say, you guys are going to hell. He just was saying how we need to be segregated, and Blacks need to be with Blacks, Mexicans need to be with Mexicans, and whites need to be with whites. I told him that is not how the world works, and he said, well, that's how I'm trying to make it. Then I said that all I can do is pray for you, he said that he's had a lot of people say that to him. Some conversations you just need to drop, because they're too jaded and corrupted.

Also, in understanding racism one must acknowledge it as a system of power (Lipsitz 1998; Omi and Winant 1994) that has the ability to affect the lives of people of Asian/black backgrounds, as was noted by Tyrone when he noticed that he was passed up on a job because of his race:

> **Tyrone (abm 28)** – After high school and a little bit of junior college, I started my first job. I went with my cousin, who is White and Samoan with straight hair and lighter skinned, but he had no experience being fresh out of high school. They called him first before me, even though I put in the application before him. They put him in an office, and they gave me some mail job. I thought I was more qualified than he was, but I ended up passing out mail. I think society does still run based on race. The place I work now, I've worked there for eight years, and I see it so much. I see people getting more bonuses than me, and I know I'm more qualified than most of them. I am looking for another job, but I haven't explained that to the owner yet. I don't think it will change even if I talk to him.

Therefore, it seems clear that many people of Asian/black backgrounds did not accept and actively fought against a constrained black identity because of the anti-black racism of society in general, but because of the racism of white people in particular. Consequently, this allows an Asian/black racial identity to be viewed as a rational racial identity. The only question left to answer in regard to a possible safe space for people of Asian/black backgrounds would be black people. In the next section, I will analyze how blackness is also socially enforced by black people, and how this process can marginalize people of Asian/black backgrounds in general, but Asian/black women specifically.

"You're Not Black Enough": Asian/Black People Who Do Not Act Black

In the past, anti-black racism from society allowed multiracial black people who were mostly of black, white and Native American heritage to solidify a positive understanding of blackness, which was a key to the development of the Harlem Renaissance and ultimately created the consciousness necessary to form the Civil Rights Movement (Davis 1991). However, when white supremacy gave ground to the racial equality paradigm, which eventually took the form of the Black Power movement of the 1960s and 1970s, race and racial identification became almost synonymous with each other (Winant 2001; Omi and Winant 1994). As Omi and Winant stated, this transformation in our socio-political sphere redefined race and added the necessary component of racial identity into the discourse:

> This expansion of "normal" politics to include racial issues—this "common sense" recognition of the political elements at the heart of racial identities and meanings—made possible the movement's greatest triumphs, its most permanent successes. These did not lie in its legislative accomplishments, but rather in its ability to create new racial "subjects." The black movement *redefined the meaning of racial identity*, and consequently of race *itself*, in American society. Social movements create collective identity by offering their adherents a different view of themselves and their world; different, that is, from the worldview and self-concepts offered by the established social order (emphasis in the original). (Omi and Winant 1995, pg. 99)

However, when racial discourse shifted to include identity, this allowed the boundaries between races to be enforced by the racial groups themselves, rather than just by the established order (Mezey 2003; Snipp 2003). Although this did not seem problematic in the beginning, as blackness became increasingly defined by black people, the social context was created as to what was considered "black enough," which had a marginalizing effect on many people of Asian/black backgrounds in my sample (Kennedy 2003; Sollors 2000; Davis 1991).

Current perceptions of black identity used both cultural and physical attributes to determine who was "black enough" (Hall and Turner 2001). However, this conceptualization of blackness created the dynamic for many people of Asian/black backgrounds to be interpreted as having an external black identity by people who were not black, while not being seen as black by other black people. Even though Sumi was born and raised in Japan and struggled with her racial identity, she made it clear that Japanese people saw her as black even though she was culturally Japanese:

> **Sumi (abf 20)** – When I was in Okinawa, the people who love Black people and loved the history about them would be more interested in me, but there were those who were not so interested in me, they would drift apart from me. It's like that for both sides. Only Japanese people who are interested in the Black culture usually draw close to me to learn more about the Black side of me.

The idea that Japanese people are now interested in black culture suggests a shift in racial thinking, however, research suggests that interest is more about consumerism than genuine interest in black culture (Cornyetz 1994).

Although having a black external racial identity has a lot to do with how Sumi looks, which she described as mostly black, when asked how other black people think, she immediately stated that black people see her as more Japanese rather than black. Sumi arrived at this conclusion herself because she observed that black people talked to her differently than they did to other black people:

> **Sumi (abf 20)** – From what people have told me, I would say slightly. Black people would put me more into the Japanese category than the Black category. They see me as way more Japanese. When they talk to me, it is a lot different than how they communicate with their other Black friends ... My friend would be more active and more excited when she talks to her other friends. She also uses a lot more slang when she's talking to them. It's probably because I don't know a lot. She is calmer when she communicates with me ... I don't mind. I know that they aren't trying to do anything on purpose or anything.

Sumi went into further detail when she made the observation that other people saw her as black because they were not as familiar with black culture, while she believed that black people could tell if someone was acting black or not:

> **Sumi (abf 20)** – I think they see me as more Black. I think it's because Black people know the Black culture and the Black feelings more than other races do. I guess they can see if I'm acting Black so they would know more than the other races. With the other races, they can see me as Black because I'm different from their cultures. Here is a Black person who knows their stuff, and they see me. They know the ways I'm acting. Here are the

other races who aren't Black; they don't know the Black culture or Japanese culture, so when they see me doing one or the other they will put me into whichever category they see.

Sumi's experiences strongly suggest that for black people, looking black was not enough; you also had to act black. This is diametrically opposed to white and Asian people where looking white or Asian was more important than how you acted. This probably has something to do with the incredibly wide range of African American phenotypes in the U.S. and that there are people that are black that are "passing" for white (Daniel 1992), and so, how closely you identify with black culture/politics is more important than how you look.

Although it would be easy to ascribe Sumi's experience to the fact that she was born and raised in Japan, Theo, who was born and raised in the United States, had a similar experience because black people thought he acted white. Theo, self-described as looking mostly black to other people, conveyed an experience where he was told by a black woman that he was the whitest black man she had ever met:

> **Theo (abm 33)** – It's just kind of hard to describe. Blacks just see me and my skin color. I had one black girl, for some reason, when I lived in D.C. she told me I was the "whitest" black guy she ever met. (laughs) I don't know what that meant, but I said, oh, thank you. Then I said, what the hell is she talking about (hushed voice)?

When asked what that meant to him, Theo suggested that black people used a lot of slang, while he spoke "properly":

> **Theo (abm 33)** – What I am thinking is that the black guys she knows talk slang and all that stuff, but me, I talk proper, you know, grammar with manners. I could be wrong, but that is what I thought it meant. It did kind of stun me, because I did not know how to take that in.

Therefore, the political shift that connected race and identification made it where looking black was not enough; you also had to act black. In other words, black people have defined blackness to encompass both phenotypic and cultural attributes, and if you looked black, but did not act black, then you were not considered black (Hall and Turner 2001).

The experiences of Sumi and Theo as they interacted with black people seem to run counter to the experiences of Mary, Ai and Tyrone with Asians, as they suggested that it was more important to *look* Asian that to *act* Asian. Rebecca Chiyoko King's research (2001) on the San Francisco Cherry Blossom Queen Pageant strongly supports that it is more important for multiracial Asians to look Asian in order to gain acceptability in an American context. King illustrates this with how Japanese-American participants did not know as much about Japanese culture, but *looked* Japanese, while Asian/white participants knew more about Japanese culture, but used heavy eyeliner to make themselves look more *Asian*. By Sumi and Theo's own admittance, they both look black; however, this begs the question as to what happens when someone who is of Asian/black heritage does not look black?

"You're Not Black Enough," Part 2: Asian/Black People Who Do Not Look Black

Although a few people of Asian/black backgrounds stated that they thought they looked mostly black to themselves and to other people, most of the people in my sample described themselves as looking somewhere in the middle regarding their facial and body features. Being something less than black, e.g., having long hair, having straight or wavy hair, having almond-shaped eyes or being petite, had a strong effect on the experiences of Asian/black women and men within the black community.

The Treatment of Asian/Black Women

Asian/black women that looked ambiguous became "exotic" to men in general, but to black men in particular, and therefore, attractive (Kennedy 2003). However, being interpreted as different by black women led to being alienated, at best, and verbally and physically abused, at worst. Finding women of Asian/black backgrounds attractive was a discernable pattern with the vast majority of black men, but Jane uncovered that these men found them attractive because they were "exotic" looking, rather than fitting into traditional understandings of black feminine beauty:

> **Jane (abf 24)** – I think black guys find me attractive. They like the long hair, light skinned, petite person ... This black guy I dated, he actually spoke Vietnamese which was interesting, and he always told me to wear my hair down because I looked more Asian that way. I was older and so I didn't conform to his wishes as much as I did with past boyfriends. So I was like, whatever, I didn't feel like doing my hair. He was not my ideal guy, but it had nothing to do with him being black.

Elizabeth found black men linked her to traditional images of black feminine beauty, but would also recognize her differences. This was most clearly seen when black men changed the words to "She's a Brick House" by the Commodores, a funk/soul/R&B group of the 1970s, when they referred to her:

> **Elizabeth (abf 48)** – Well, in California, the men I dated were predominately black men. They liked the fact that I had long hair, and the Commodores had a song called "Brick House," and they used to call me a little brick shithouse. (laughs) I have always had the legs, but people would always say that my ass was the black side of me.

Black men referred to her as a brick house, which fell within traditional black feminine beauty, but the addition of "little" and "shithouse" was used to recognize her overall petite frame with the notable exception of her butt. However, being labeled as exotic made Margaret feel "alien" rather than beautiful:

> **Margaret (abf 46)** – I had a teacher once that told me in high school that I look pretty darn good "considering." That was a psychology teacher in high school ... Considering that I was half black and half Japanese, I guess I look pretty darn good. That's how I took it and that's how he meant it. I'm not a monster ... I mean, I don't look like a bizarre alien, but "considering." (laughs) It's like, considering you're a girl, you play sports well. Meaning you can't just play sports, because you're a girl. "Considering" I'm this weird taboo, I look pretty darn good. Anyways, I just laugh it off because people say weird things to me every day.

Therefore, Margaret saw through the "exotic" label as one that connoted beauty, but most importantly was that it signified difference.

Although being seen as exotic by black men was a benefit, being different to black women caused serious social interaction problems. Reiko spoke of how she has tried to get along with other black women, but that they have not accepted her because of her differences:

> **Reiko (abf 20)** – One day I figured it wasn't working that way, and my grandmother would yell at me that I embrace my Japanese side more than my black side. But I told her that I'm not really well accepted on that side. I'm proud that I'm half black. I do what I have to do to be half black, or whatever, but I'm not comfortable and obviously they're not very comfortable. We don't hate each other, it's just I don't fit into that group and that's okay.

This difference, as noted by Aiko, always started with the hair (Hall and Turner 2001; Root 2001). When asked about whether black people accepted her or not, Aiko originally stated that she was completely accepted, but had to change her assessment because she had blocked out how badly black women have treated her:

> **Aiko (abf 35)** – Yes, black people love me, especially black men.
>
> **Interviewer** – So nothing with black women?
>
> **Aiko (abf 35)** – Well, of course they don't like me. (laughs) I guess I was only thinking of black men. Black women do not like me; my God, they don't like me. They would call me halfbreed; they would say I think I'm too good. It was based on jealousy. I dated two black men, and when I've done that black women treat me nasty. When I was young and went to church, I had hair past my butt and my mom would put it in two ponytails, and the black girls would pull my hair and say halfbreed. They would pick on me and my sister a lot because we weren't full black.

The issue of hair in the African American community is of extreme importance:

> In African cultures, the grooming and styling of hair have long been important social rituals. Elaborate hair designs, reflecting tribal affiliation, status, sex, age, occupation, and the like were common, and the cutting, shaving, wrapping, and braiding of hair were centuries-old arts. (White and White 1995, p. 49)

And the hair of black women has been used to symbolize freedom and self-appreciation in many acclaimed novels by black women (Weitz 2001; Ashe 1995). Therefore, I argue that the negative association of women of Asian/black backgrounds and their wavy, rather than kinky, hair is symbolic of their lack of black authenticity as perceived by black people in general, but black women specifically.

The idea that Asian/black women thought they were better than black women was also shared by Elizabeth, who was continuously verbally and physically assaulted by young black women because of her differences:

> **Elizabeth (abf 46)** – I remember being about twelve or thirteen and going to school in Oklahoma, and I remember all the little kids not knowing what I was or who I am. So they would pull their eyes tight and call me "ching-chong." There were two black girls that would follow me home everyday from school, but keep about six paces behind me, and on weekends they would wait outside behind the bushes or the trees and wait for me to come outside so that they could pounce on me, or intimidate me more. It came to the point where I would be walking home from school and they would be walking behind me, and my father would be driving very slowly behind them. Once they actually chased me home into my house, and my stepmother was mopping the floor and she ran them out. Since I was younger, I have always been ridiculed by black people.

All of the Asian/black women in my sample were proud of being black, but the ill treatment they received by black people in general, but black women specifically, caused many to not develop an internal black identity. Aiko spoke about how the sum total of her experiences had influenced her to just state that she was Japanese when people asked her about her race:

> **Aiko (abf 35)** – Now that I think about it, in my experience black people have been more prejudice to me than anyone. Black girls were prejudice to me here, but just black people in general in the Midwest. Maybe that's why I don't care for certain black people. This may sound prejudice, but I can see one as they're walking towards me because of how they walk or how they dress. And when they talk to you they always make it a point to tell you who they are as if you can't relate, like I'm black and I'm proud. And I'm okay with that and always give people a chance, but there's so much more than just being black, and maybe since I've never been given a chance I just don't get into that issue very much. Now that I think about it, I always say I'm Japanese and I never say I'm black. But to me that's just obvious, so I don't state it.

Although these experiences told us what happened, they have not told us why it happened. Many Asian/black women stated that black women were jealous (Kennedy 2003), but what created the jealousy? Jane hinted at what the origin of this jealousy might be when she spoke of how one of her black female friends always commented on her beauty:

> **Jane (abf 24)** – I have a friend who's black, well, actually her mom is white and her dad is black, but she really doesn't identify with the white side and she's sweet. She would always say, you're

so lucky that your hair grows long. She would say you're black but you're very pretty. She was always very complimentary of how I looked. I don't think black women looked at me negatively, I don't know. I guess I would think more about it if there were more black people around.

The fact that Jane referred to her friend as black, even though her friend was of multiracial white/black heritage, clearly demonstrated how people of white/black heritage are still considered black (Davis 1991). More importantly, her friend being understood as black added meaning to when her friend said, "You're black but you're very pretty." This statement suggested that black women have, to whatever degree, internalized whiteness as the standard of beauty, and therefore, have placed themselves on the bottom of the beauty hierarchy (Collins 2000; Hooks 1981).

The Treatment of Asian/Black Men

Although not looking black was a problem that both Asian/black women and men faced, men gained a huge social advantage to fitting in if they were good at sports (Messner 1992). Tim observed that his team used racial humor as a method of socialization, and that the multiple races of his baseball team came together as they played other teams with more homogeneous compositions who made racist comments toward members of his team:

> **Tim (abm 41)** – I had a lot of friends of different races, and we made fun of each other but it was always within the group. We were comfortable calling each other names, but it would be more threatening if it were someone outside of the group. We use racial humor to socialize on. For example, on my baseball team we were a lot of different races, but then we would play against another team that was just one race. And you would hear from that one race about all of our different races. I've mentioned rice ball and I never heard that in my family before, and when I played against other teams they would make that my nickname. I would think to myself, I like rice and everything, but why do they have to call me that? They were trying to get down on me, and I took it as a defensive thing. People that want to make fun of my race is a defensive thing. So that was my analysis of that. Even my friends got called pineapple, banana, spear chucker or whatever, and I defended that, but in their group they were defensive because they were only one race and so that's all they knew. So we played with that, we listened to that, we took that in, but we never got physical over it because there was no reason for that.

Tim also noticed that the better they did, the worse the crowd taunted them:

> **Tim (abm 41)** – We never threw anything back at them, what we threw back at them was our talent and our ability to play. So the better we did, the more we would hear from them. Not only from them, but also their families sitting in the stands, they would even write signs that said things like "go back home". Yeah, we were talking late 70s, early 80s, but we did what we knew and that was play the game.

Being good at sports provided Tim with a productive outlet to deal with the vile, racist taunts of the crowds, and made the team conscious of how they taught new team members about race:

> **Tim (abm 41)** – We were damn good! (laughs) We had a lot of good talent back then, but it was nothing to brag about. It helped us with our self-esteem, and it was a confidence you kept it yourself rather than worry about race because you were a team. A half black, half Japanese pitcher throwing to a Hawaiian/Chinese/Portuguese catcher with a white first baseman and a black shortstop, but you didn't even think about that. But the opponents did, and they would see it and use it against you. We just thought that it was not part of our game and nothing to get down about. If anyone new came to our team who was unfamiliar with that, they would get educated real quick.

Therefore, Tim and his baseball team learned that winning was the answer for racism.

Playing sports was beneficial to the development of good race relations amongst team members, but playing sports did not make a team colorblind. As a matter of fact, it made it more colorful as teammates made racial jokes and nicknames. This was noted by Tyrone, whose teammates made nicknames for multiracial players:

> **Tyrone (abm 28)** – In high school, we had a couple guys who were White and Filipino and Black and Filipino on the team; they had nicknames for everyone. White and Filipinos were "flights" and I was a "fligger." Just names like that because guys do that. I don't think it was on purpose racially, though.

The appreciation of diversity within sports may have something to do with how sports are structured. Most team sports have discernable positions that have very specific qualities and attributes. Therefore, playing sports magnified differences, but also demonstrated how differences were incorporated into a single team.

Sports proved to benefit Asian/black men, as it regarded social acceptance, but it also had the effect of developing a constrained black identity. Reggie commented on how he supported black players because they are a "dying breed":

> **Reggie (abm 22)** – I don't like to put people in categories, like he's Black because he dresses this way, or he listens to this kind of music. I just think it is how you think of yourself. You don't need a label with it. But at the same time, I do look up to Black athletes and Black musicians ... Because they are good and because they are Black, for example, in baseball, Blacks in baseball are a dying breed, and I try to support them however I can to try to get that back. I feel like that should be stronger for the community.

When asked to go into more detail, Reggie explained that there was a bond amongst black players because there were so few:

> **Reggie (abm 22)** – I'm looking for myself to get up in the ranks, but I'm also rooting for other guys too. It's a different special bond that we have because there are so few of us. I only had one on my team last year, and everybody else was either white or Latin.

Although sports in general made socialization and fitting in easier for Asian/black men, the racial dynamics of the sport could also create a bond between black players and draw them closer to a black identity.

Conclusion

In summary, race has had a detrimental effect on the assimilation process, as racial categories are (re)negotiated, (re)examined and (re)defined through the experiences of people of Asian/white and Asian/black backgrounds. The multiracial project has allowed the reestablishment of white supremacy through the minimizing of Asian heritage by people of Asian/white backgrounds. One way that this was shown was in the fact that people of Asian/white backgrounds in my sample were more likely to state that they had a white racial identification than people of Asian/black backgrounds were to identify as being black. This strongly suggests that, although constrained, there was a social advantage connected to a white racial identity.

Our current racial order was also (re)established through the (re)enforcement of black inferiority through the racist treatment of people of Asian/black backgrounds from people of all races, including black people. Although they were of Asian/black backgrounds, Asian and white people most often treated them like they were just black by calling them nigger or treating them inferiorly at a job. However, some of the most racist attitudes and behaviors towards people of Asian/black backgrounds came from black people themselves who saw them as "not black enough." Also, some of the most physical abuse came from black women towards women of Asian/black backgrounds because of the internalization of black inferiority, and led these women to push away from a black identity. This negativity allowed for the creation of a rational multiracial identity for people of Asian/black backgrounds.

Although Asian/black women were verbally, emotionally and physically abused by all members of society, Asian/black men who were good at sports had an altogether different experience as it pertained to fitting in socially. Sports allowed for these men to bond with other races of people and to acknowledge and appreciate the differences amongst them. Also, racial dynamics on and off the field had the tendency to pull Asian/black men towards a black identity.

5
Learning Racial Hierarchy

One of the most common notions regarding the seeming explosion of interracial marriage is that this signifies the acceptance of people of color into the white American mainstream (Patterson 1997; Hollinger 1995). This idea is supported by assimilation theorists who follow the ethnicity model for race relations and suggest that as European ethnics eventually melted together to form what we now understand as white people, so now will people of color blend together with white people and become Americans. Although this is a common understanding of how race will be absorbed within the assimilation process, this chapter will ask two questions that will challenge the major assumptions of this paradigm: is the assimilation process alone the best way to understand the high interracial marriage rates of Asians? And, are interracial couples less likely than the rest of society to hold onto notions of racial hierarchy, which will be the driving question for this chapter.

Interracial Marriage and the Assimilation Process

Can Assimilation Alone Explain Interracial Marriage with Asians?

Hwang, Saenez and Aguirre, in their article, "Structural and Assimilationist Explanations of Asian American Intermarriage," conducted research in order to figure out how the assimilation process has affected Asian American interracial marriage patterns. What was initially found was that English fluency was a major factor contributing to interracial marriage with Asians, which suggests that the increase in interracial marriages with Asian Americans is due to the acculturation process of assimilation. The assimilation position was strengthened by the association of more intermarriages occurring with Asians who immigrated to the U.S. before 1965, thus concluding that interracial marriages are more likely once cultural barriers are removed.

However, the authors also found that the higher an Asian person's education levels are, the less likely they were to interracially marry, which they could not explain with an assimilationist or structuralist framework. Although they could not reconcile this seeming contradiction, the authors concluded that, "Our evidence provides overwhelming support to the claim that high acculturation leads to more intermarriage" (p. 770). However, I argue that an explanation that places race at the center of analysis can be used to explain this seeming contradiction and produce a more fluid and consistent model.

Connecting the context of most interracial marriages occurring amongst Asians that have arrived in the U.S. before 1965, places this population within a war bride context rather than an assimilationist framework. This assertion is strengthened by the fact that the vast majority of people in interracial marriages were born in foreign countries rather than in the United States (Saenez et al. 1994; Thornton 1992). Although current studies show that American-born Asians are more likely to intermarry than foreign-born (Liang and Ito 1999), placing Asian interracial marriages within a war bride setting allows the comparison that 60 percent of foreign-born Japanese women interracially marry, in general, in comparison to only 25 percent of their U.S. born counterparts (Jacobs and Labov 2002). If this is the case, one would then have to conclude that fluency in English is relative to a pre-assimilation context and not an educational context, and suggests that there is something about a United States' environment that lessens the chance of people of Asian heritage to interracially marry.

With this new understanding, the difference between educational level and interracial marriage must be re-examined. If Asians with higher education levels have a higher ethnic identification (Xie and Goyette 1997) and are less likely to interracially marry, this strongly suggests that the assimilation process of the United States actually strengthens understandings of racial categories, not lessens them. If understood in this manner, then any argument regarding social distance and interracial marriage must be understood as a *combination* of socio-economic status (Kuo 1970) and racial status within the U.S.

An examination of interracial marriage statistics strongly suggests that these marriages follow our current racial hierarchy with black people being grossly underrepresented in the statistics of who intermarries. Of the six major Asian ethnicities in the United States, interracial marriage amongst black people was about 1.5 percent of the total marriages of foreign-born Asians, while whites represented approximately 27 percent (Le 2006). This suggests that foreign-born Asians are approximately eighteen times more likely to interracially marry someone who is white versus someone who is black. Of Asian Americans this number increases even further with black people representing approximately 2.3 percent of interracial marriages with Asian Americans, while whites are approximately 52 percent (Ibid.). This suggests that Asian Americans are about twenty-two times more likely to marry someone white rather than black. Since black people represent about 13 percent and non-Hispanic white people represent about 67 percent of the U.S. population, the probability of an Asian person marrying a white person over a black person should statistically be only five times greater (U.S. Census 2000). Therefore, what this suggests is that the color line is being (re)established within the context of who marries interracially, and who does not.

Although this huge disparity exists, the multiracial project keeps society focused on how interracial marriages have "dramatically" increased since the Supreme Court decided that anti-miscegenation laws were unconstitutional in 1967 (Johnson 2003; Williams-Leon and Nakashima 2001; Root 1996) in order to lead us away from the fact that racial hierarchy is manifesting itself within the patterns of interracial marriage. Therefore, this chapter will examine how the people of Asian/white and Asian/black backgrounds in my sample learned about race and racial hierarchy within their family structures.

It Starts in the Home

When speaking about race and racism, most people would state that it starts in the home. Therefore, the next part of this examination will analyze the parents to uncover how color lines become visible and are established within family and peer relationships, and whether their experiences fit an assimilationist framework.

Throughout my study, it was made clear that Asian cultures in general did not condone, and at times, actively condemned, interracial marriages with Americans of any race. This has to do mostly with the relationship of Americans as a military presence in Asian countries and the inherent power relationship between these forces (Enloe 2000; Thornton 1992). Although this is true of all interracial relationships with Asian people, notions of racial hierarchy emerge within the context of how interracial couples were treated by their parents and peers. Whiteness often afforded a pathway that was acceptable, even if it was not particularly appreciated by immediate family members. However, this was not the case with being married to someone who was black, where immediate family members often vehemently enforced the notion of the unsuitability of black people as marriage partners.

Although the military experience fits four of the six sets of parents that I interviewed and almost all of the multiracial respondents, I will start this section with an examination of the difference between how Asian and white and Asian and black interracial couples are treated when all members were raised in the United States. Then, I will later discuss the racial ramifications of an Asian woman, foreign-born/military American male context.

The two American-raised couples are important to deeply examine for numerous control-related reasons. For one, these two couples are in the *opposite* pattern of the vast majority of my sample, because both of my couples had an Asian male as the husband, and the wife was either white or black. Both men are of Chinese heritage, both are highly educated, and neither was directly involved with the military.

When We First Met

Melvin and Alexandria

When speaking of how these two couples met, it is important to understand the socio-political context in which they grew up. The ages of Melvin, Alexandria, Rosie and Ted allowed them to experience most, if not all, of the countercultural revolution that happened during the sixties and seventies (Spates 1976). Therefore, the belief in non-traditional couples may have been in the minds of Melvin, a 52-year-old Asian male, and Alexandria, a 49-year-old white female, when they met each other at the wedding of a mutual friend:

> **Alexandria (wfp[1] 49)** – I met him at my best friend's wedding, and he was in the wedding, he was one of the groomsmen. I remember his smile mostly. I wasn't introduced to him; I just went through the reception line.

And then a chance phone call to a friend's parents' house while Melvin was housesitting led to them going on their first date together at a Christian music concert:

> **Alexandria (wfp 49)** – I told him why I was calling, and we talked about political and church stuff. He mentioned he was going to concerts at church. I had always wanted to go, but didn't want to drive to Orange County by myself. I wanted to go with friends, but we ended up going by ourselves. We were both just

brave enough to go as friends. It was Christian music with a Bible study afterward.

Rosie and Ted

Although Melvin and Alexandria met in a seemingly race neutral manner, race was at the center of how Rosie, a 65-year-old black female, and Ted, a 64-year-old Asian male, met each other as they worked for the American Friends Service Group:

> **Rosie (bfp[2] 65)** – It was in the summer after I graduated college and moved to California to be with the American Friends Service Group. It was different groups from all around who came to be one big group in California. It was there that everyone was introduced and found out about the project we were doing for the summer. I don't remember the first meeting; only that everybody was friendly and so was he. I don't have anything clear in my mind on a first meeting.

The American Friends Service Group, founded in 1917, was a Quaker organization that focused on social justice and equality, and won a Nobel Peace Prize in 1947 (Nobelprize.org). So from the start, Rosie and Ted's relationship began within the context of an organization that had a high racial awareness and a desire to create social equality. Ted went further by saying that he developed his current social awareness because of an event that he attended in his youth that was associated with the same group, which he believed allowed him to be open-minded enough to eventually marry his wife:

> **Ted (amp[3] 64)** – One of the formative events in my life was in the summer of my freshman year of high school. I went to a thing called Anytown, which is run by the National Conference of Christians and Jews. The whole organization began in 1937. They used to be the organization that ran Brotherhood Week. I went in 1958 that summer, and it was a camp. It might have been called an encounter group for high school teenagers. It lasted a week in the mountains in Prescott, Arizona. They took student leaders and put us together to talk about issues of race, religion and ethnicity. I was not socially aware. That summer I had a different look into the world. I think it led me to study psychology instead of engineering. So Anytown was a very important turning point for me. My wife and I about five years ago were counselors for an event. I think I had a better understanding of people and racism by then. I was excited about people who were culturally, socially and religiously different than I.

Anytown, a residential youth leadership program, was established in 1950 and was sponsored by the National Conference for Christians and Jews, a human relations organization dedicated to fighting bias and racism in the United States (NCCJ 2002). It was this experience that allowed Ted to study psychology rather than engineering, and put him on the path to eventually meet his wife.

Even the first real date between Rosie and Ted involved race as they watched *Westside Story*, a love story that crossed racial lines:

> **Rosie (bfp 65)** – A few of us lived on the grounds where we worked. We would get together to do social things, but it wasn't boy and girl deal, just in a group. Then from that we just talked as friends, and then we became really close friends. At some point he asked me to go out, and we went to see *West Side Story*. We had fun together, but it wasn't serious like boyfriend/girlfriend; we just knew we enjoyed each other's company. Then we started going out more to dinners and movies, and it got pretty serious then. It just grew from there.

Family, Friends and Interracial Marriage

Melvin and Alexandria

As things blossomed, I asked Melvin to tell me how his family and friends felt about his interracial relationship, and he immediately began talking about how his dating was affected by his physical location:

> **Melvin (amp 52)** – I don't think they had a problem with it. We originally were from Gardenia, and there were a lot of Japanese people there. All my friends were Japanese. We moved from there to Torrance which was an all Caucasian area. There weren't many Japanese.

Melvin, who was fourth generation Chinese American, spoke about his Japanese friends, and how "... all of my friends were Japanese" strongly suggested that he and his friends had developed a pan-Asian identity (Espiritu 1992). Although Espiritu fully explained that physical similarity amongst Asian people did not create a primordial sense of community within Asia, she made it clear that these similarities helped create a definite experience within the United States as Asian people.

However, primordial understandings of race were affirmed through Melvin's own explanation about why he became friends with people of Japanese heritage, and how he had never had a problem with Japanese people:

> **Melvin (amp 52)** – "I don't know, probably because we look similar!"

This statement completely neglected to address the historical legacy between Japanese and Chinese people in Asia and in the United States in favor of a racial explanation as to why these two groups seemingly got along so well. This assertion further (re)enforced the understanding that physical similarities build community, rather than cultural or individual attributes.

Melvin maintained that the physical limitations of who he dated and married as the primary reason why no one, including his parents, had a problem with it:

> **Melvin (amp 52)** – After high school, most of my friends were White. They didn't think anything of it. My parents didn't think anything of it either because that was all that was around. I have three cousins who married Chinese people. Basically, our family is pretty mixed. My brothers are both married to Caucasian women.

This formulation of "I just married who was around" is important to note because it allows for someone to eliminate the idea that they chose *not* to marry someone of a different race other than those that were around. This construction also negates the reality of racial segregation in order to create an innocence regarding why his parents may have moved into that area in the first place (Frankenberg 1993).

Rosie and Ted
For Rosie and Ted, things were different. Once it got serious, that was when notions of racial hierarchy came into play, even with their close friends:

> **Ted (amp 64)** – You asked me about my friends. I had one friend tell me that what I planned to do was a bad idea. About ten years later he married a Black woman, and he's White. (laughs) At the time, he thought it was going to ruin my life. In general, people thought we were just young. In terms of our colleagues, they were surprised we got married. It just wasn't the thing to do. Dating was bad enough, but getting married made people ask, what are you doing? Our friends did support us, though.

This seems like the expected response given that Rosie and Ted probably met before anti-miscegenation laws were deemed unconstitutional. However, this is an interesting observation considering the radical political time frame they grew up in, which suggests how deeply racial notions regarding who was proper marriage material were ingrained.

By placing everyone's concerns within a socio-historical context, Ted creates a sense of innocence regarding the people involved, which also happened with Alexandria later in this section. Ted used it to illustrate his point and connect larger social factors to his eventual marriage. His white friend literally thought that Ted would ruin his life if he married a black woman, but eventually married a black woman himself. This clearly demonstrates how the concept of race has shaped black people to be viewed as the bottom rung of society.

Rosie talks about how difficult it was to make African American friends because of having an Asian husband:

> **Rosie (bfp 65)** – I base that on attempts to make social connections with women. They would be nice, but if they got together to do certain things I wasn't invited. We would invite Afro-American couples to dinner at our house, and some would reciprocate and some didn't. I think it had a lot to do with not knowing anything about the Chinese culture. They, Black males, didn't know how to relate to Ted.

In this situation, it is not Ted's race that Rosie considered, but his culture. However, it seemed clear from the context of the quote that African Americans were also making racial assumptions about Asian Americans. Interestingly enough, these types of complications were anticipated from the start, but the confidence of youth prevailed:

> **Rosie (bfp 65)** – We set out to conquer the world, and we did. We felt very confident and naïve and young. It was to our advantage because if we had been smarter, we would've thought it out. We just went on, though. I remember working at a children's house, and this girl told me that marriage was too complicated to mix race or religion. She said it like she really believed it too. Over the years, I wish she could see me now.

This youthful confidence also can be a product of the times, as America's youth rebelled against authority and attempted to change the world (Smiley 1977).

Parental Establishment of the Color Line

Rosie and Ted

Although friends seemed skeptical and hesitant, they remained supportive, but the parents proved to be much harsher in their dealings. Rosie, who knew that her mother would probably disapprove, decided to wait until after she and Ted had eloped to tell her mother:

> **Rosie (bfp 65)** – I figure she disapproved, which she did. I thought if I told her beforehand that she would try to stop it from happening. I went ahead and did it because once it's done, it can't be undone. (laughs).

When asked if her mother's disapproval was racially based, Rosie stated that it was, but more so because of the lack of knowledge of Asian Americans at the time, rather than an overarching ideology of Asian American unsuitability for marriage:

> **Rosie (bfp 65)** – Initially, yeah, because she didn't have any concept of who this person was or anything. In life I think you are always more afraid of the unknown. Race probably entered into it, because if I just up and married an Afro-American man, that would have been the end of it. So the shock was the marriage as well as a marriage outside of the race.

Ted remembered Rosie's mother's first question after finding out he was Chinese: which side would he be on if the U.S. and China go to war:

> **Ted (amp 64)** – When Roz told her mother, her first question was if America and China go to war, which side would I be on? That was five or six years after the Korean War, and the Cold War was heating up. She did support us in all ways, though. Her Black friends were supportive.

In questioning his allegiance, Rosie's mother demonstrated a political consciousness grounded in racially essentialist notions that Asians were somehow super-patriotic (Smythe 1953), but after some time she did manage to support the newlyweds.

Although racial hierarchy did not seem to be at the center of Rosie's mother's disapproval, it definitely was at the center for Ted's parents. As a matter of fact, Ted knew that the consequences of marrying a black woman would be so severe that he purposely did not tell his parents that he was married for several years:

> **Ted (amp 64)** – My parents didn't know until after we got married. When they found out, not from my help, they disowned me. My father called and said he didn't want to see me, and if he did he'd kill me. My siblings were supportive, and I got calls from them. My family has seven children; five are my half brothers and sisters, and I have a full sister. My full sister found out, wasn't happy, but afterward accepted it. My father and stepmom were totally against it. My brothers and sisters were too young, but my oldest younger brother called and said he supported me.

Ted then goes on to explain how racial hierarchy worked for Chinese people: if you are not Chinese, then you are a barbarian:

> **Ted (amp 64)** – In China, there are only Chinese people. There are no Black people or White people. It's a homogeneous country. I remember when I was young, there were comments about the Indians in Hong Kong. The Indians were darker than the Chinese. China is so big. It's not that integrated; Chinese people are very ethnocentric. Their words for people who aren't Chinese are barbarians. White people we call "white devils" and Black people we call "black devils" or "Mr. Ink."

However, Ted did make it clear that his parents did not approve of him marrying outside of his race in general, but a black woman specifically:

> **Ted (amp 64)** – My parents were upset because I married someone who was not Chinese, and especially someone who was Black. Totally not acceptable … They would've been upset if I married a White woman. In fact, my brother married a White woman and was able to keep it a secret for three years. The family wasn't supportive at all. They didn't re-own me for twelve years.

Although being interracially married was bad in any context, it can be inferred by the text of his brother's experience that if Ted married a white woman that he would not have been disowned by his family. This situation clearly demonstrated the privileging of whiteness even within communities of color.

When asked if his parents brought a pre-existing color line from China, Ted stated that was not the case. He suggested that his parents internalized the racial structure of the U.S. in order to put black people at the bottom of the racial hierarchy:

> **Ted (amp 64)** – It's not China, it's here. My dad was in the U.S. Army, and after the war, he brought my sister and me since my

mom died when I was six months old. We went to Tucson, Arizona where my dad owned a grocery store. There was racism toward Black, Latino and Whites. They understood the social structure; Blacks were worse off than Latinos who were worse off than Whites. From the viewpoint, they adopted the social standards of racism.

This is consistent with interracial marriage statistics and how these mirror the color line of the United States (Le 2006).

Fascinatingly enough, as well-established notions of white suitability for interracial marriage were set in his parents, Ted somehow convinced Rosie that their experiences with his parents were not based on race, but on nationality:

> **Rosie (bfp 65)** – I thought it was, but Ted said not. I believe him because later he had a brother who married a White woman. The reaction was not as strong, but my brother-in-law, he married this person, he didn't tell his family for five years. I realized then it wasn't because I'm this color, it is because I'm not Chinese.

Despite Rosie's disbelief, this color line maintains itself even through the reconciliation process with Ted's parents through a lack of admission of racist thinking. So when asked if his father ever forgave him, Ted was not overwhelmed with the forgiveness of his father:

> **Ted (amp 64)** – More or less. I married Rosie in 1963; I got my doctorate in 1968. We went east to Pennsylvania and then came here. In 1975, my brother, dad and mom asked to come down for a visit. It was very awkward; we talked, and he asked if we could come to a dinner in Chinatown. That is Chinese speak for, we have a banquet, and now you are forgiven. It wasn't anything I did; they decided I didn't ruin my life after all.

Melvin and Alexandria
Notions of racial hierarchy become apparent as Alexandria's mother demonstrated a heightened concern for her future choice in a husband from the start. When asked about how her mother felt about her dating practices, Alexandria stated that her mother was concerned because she regularly dated black men:

> **Alexandria (wfp 49)** – Well, they were probably relieved. Before I was a Christian, I was dating notorious Black men. (laughs) When I was younger, I ran away to Inglewood, so there you go. Inglewood was mainly Black people, and I made friends there.

The seemingly innocent line about her not being a Christian while dating black men suggested that her sexual morality was moderated by her whiteness (Collins 2000; Davis 1981; Hooks 1981); therefore, dating black men was somehow immoral because she did that when she was not a "Christian." The other thing to take note of in this quote was how race was spatially located with her assertion about running away to Inglewood and how that explains her relationships with black people. But the question remains, what exactly were they relieved about?

Alexandria continued to speak of how her mother felt when she thought that she was going to marry a black man, and tied that into how her parents felt relieved that she married someone with lighter skin:

> **Alexandria (wfp 49)** – I dated a Black guy for a long time, and my mom didn't want me to marry him because it looked like I might. I've always liked Black guys, so my mom was real happy when I found someone with lighter skin ... She knew at the time, in the 70s, there was prejudice. She would ask me what if I had children, what it would be like for them. You're already getting enough stares, because interracial dating is not well accepted. It was not that she was prejudice, because she wasn't. She raised me that it wasn't a big deal. But as far as dating someone of a different race, especially when there was such a distinct difference, she thought it would be really hard for me and my kids. And that was a time when it would have been, but in California I don't think it is now.

By putting her mother's comments within a socio-historical context, Alexandria tried to justify her mother's angst as parental concern and not as prejudice or racism. Concerns about her daughter's interracial relationships were not a trivial matter during this time period, because bans against interracial marriages were deemed as unconstitutional only in 1967. This largely explained why her mother was concerned about the stares of the general public in regards to her interracial dating.

However, Alexandria's mother's notions of whiteness become clearer when she took note of the assumed experiences of the children. Race was seen as so important in our society that people that are "mixed" are seen as being *between* the two groups rather than *of* both groups (Williams 1996; C. Hall 1992). Therefore, multiracial children were seen as marginalized because of their assumed inability to "fit in." However, one must realize that this concern was rather new within the social construction of race. With the "one drop rule" firmly in place for the large majority of United States history, issues regarding the children of interracial unions, whether coerced or not, were relatively simple; the child was of the minority group (Nagashima 1992; Spickard 1992; Davis 1991).

However, Howard Winant stated that racial discourse had shifted from a purely white supremacy model to a paradoxical model that incorporates both white supremacy and racial equality after WWII (Winant 2001). The move towards a racial equality paradigm created the link between race and identity through the various power movements of the 1970s, which was when Alexandria's mother made her comments about her concerns about the children, and suggested that her mother was concerned about what this *new* reality of multiracial people would be like.

Also, Alexandria privileged whiteness in the previous statement by saying that being in a black and white interracial union was not so noticeable today in California. To make this statement, Alexandria had to equalize black and white with Asian and white interracial marriages. By equating these experiences, Alexandria does not acknowledge the existence of an overarching color line that placed white and black at the poles and Asian somewhere in between (Kowner 2000). Therefore, to equalize the experiences of interracial black and white couples with Asian and white couples does not fully acknowledge the difference that society places on each union and, in essence, negates them. In other words, if someone from a black and white interracial marriage states how many problems they might have because one of them is black, Alexandria might negate the difference because she believes her experiences are directly equivalent, and she has not had similar experiences.

Alexandria also revealed her understanding of race and skin color when I asked her to explain what was so distinctly different between white and black people:

> **Alexandria (wfp 49)** – Like the contrast in color. People notice the opposite on the color wheel and pick up on it more. When we're walking down the street, and we see a Chinese and White couple, we might not notice, but if we see a Black and White couple, we notice that pretty quickly.

This quote revealed how the difference between white and black in our society has been emphasized, and how important skin color was to her regarding proposed similarities. The juxtaposing of Chinese and white and black and white couples clearly demonstrates how whiteness, and by default, lightness, was privileged in our society.

The color line was more clearly drawn by Alexandria's father, who made it clear what he thought of black people:

> **Alexandria (wfp 49)** – I think growing up my dad would tell me to not play the "nigger music," and it was mostly Jimmy Hendrix at the time. I think it was that whole time period that drove him crazy, though. It wasn't necessarily black music that drove him crazy; it was the beat, the way the songs were sung, drug music, and it was that whole time period that he associated with black people.

The construction of white innocence seems necessary and all-encompassing for Alexandria as she speaks of both of her parents. By trying to construct her father's disdain towards black people as a product of the times, she was completely disregarding how her father connected these concepts in his mind: I do not like this music, therefore, it is *nigger* music. In other words, Alexandria's father connected not liking black people to a particular genre of music, which must mean that he did not like black people regardless of what music they produced.

What About the Children?

Melvin and Alexandria
The privileging of whiteness and notions of racial hierarchy eventually translated to how their children learned about race in the household. When asked how race was discussed in his household, Melvin stated that he did not do it at all except for one time he pointed out an Asian and white family to his daughter:

> **Melvin (amp 52)** – I don't think we ever discussed it. One time my daughter and I were at a Chinese restaurant, and we saw a family where the dad was Chinese and the mom was Caucasian. They had two girls that looked half-and-half, and they had two babies. I made mention to my daughter, and she said she didn't care and that there are a lot of half-and-half people. And I was like, I just thought it was special, like you're special. Other than that, we didn't talk about race.

In this seemingly warm father/daughter moment, race was reified and whiteness was privileged. This was done through equating Asian and white to special, like his daughter. However, this construction begs the question of what interracial relationship would *not* be special? Would he have made that comment if the woman was Asian and the man was white? Would he have equated being black and Asian with being special?

Alexandria also reified race when talking to her children about who they should marry by assuming that they would marry a white or a Chinese person:

> **Alexandria (wfp 49)** – Well, the only times it came up was when I told my children that if they married a Chinese boy/girl, we'd have Chinese grandbabies, but if they marry a White boy/girl, they would look like White babies. (laughs) It was a couple of times.

So people who are Asian and white can be expected to marry someone who was either Asian *or* white, not something else. What Alexandria did not admit nor acknowledge was that if her initial construction were true, then she would not have married her Asian husband because she was white.

The privileging of whiteness can be seen through her statement that religion, not race, was the most important thing that they want for their children:

> **Alexandria (wfp 49)** – As they got older, it was only about being a Christian. I don't care if he's black, blue or green, he or she needs to be Christian, and he could even be short. (laughs) Being a Christian is a big deal for us. Race becomes a non-issue if they're a Christian.

The process of connecting being black to completely foreign concepts of blue or green for a person's skin color privileges whiteness by suggesting that black is as foreign to her as a blue or green person would be. This construction, because I have heard it many times before, makes me wish that I could do an experiment and paint someone blue or green to see if skin color really does not matter. Also, the last sentence that race is not an issue if a person is Christian strongly suggests that race is an issue if the person is *not* a Christian. Connecting this with her assumptions regarding the races of her children's possible partners, it can be deduced that being Chinese or white is automatically acceptable; however, any other race would *have* to be Christian to be acceptable.

Rosie and Ted
Although race was not a strong factor in how Melvin and Alexandria raised their children, such incredible racial and racist experiences led to Rosie and Ted being concerned about how their children were going to

be raised and treated in the places that they decided to live, due in part to their three sons' racial ambiguity:

> **Ted (amp 64)** – You didn't know they were Black. My oldest son looks like he's Polynesian. And then there's my other two sons. People probably thought they were Asian of some sort. It's not clear on what sort. People ask what they are. Some people still come up to my youngest and speak Spanish ... When my son was at the college dorm at Santa Cruz, and he had a picture of Rosie and me, and a friend of his, who was Black, said he didn't know his mom was a "sista." I guess it's not clear.

Although this was a concern, Rosie and Ted never had a "race talk" like parents have a "sex talk," which allowed them to instill what was necessary to be good people, rather than focus on their race:

> **Ted (amp 64)** – We decided to raise them as good people. They understood it at the level they could. At some point, my son was watching *Star Trek*, and he realized Mr. Sulu was Chinese. We had Chinese food. Our children were exposed to, here's mom and dad, and we're different from everyone else. We talked about race in the extent that was necessary. Race wasn't talked about as you would talk about crossing the street safely. It's not like, here's race in the U.S.; how do you talk about race to a five-year-old or even a ten-year-old? If they had questions, we responded, but there was never a "race talk" like there was a "sex talk."

Not talking to their children about race, even though they both acknowledged how problematic it could be, is a little troubling to me, but this was probably the result of a time when the concept of parenting was much less involved than how it is understood today. Even without discussing race with their children, Rosie did state clearly that she was always looking for signs of discrimination from their sons, but never saw it:

> **Rosie (bfp 65)** – It was one of those things we talked about as it came up. We were both looking for any signs of the children being harassed or teased or singled out because of their looks. The fact that we were in college communities, it tended to be more accepting. Even the parents, who didn't work at the college, seemed to be influenced by the college community and were accepting too.

Although well-intentioned, the lack of any racial dialogue with their children created some ambiguity and confusion about their children's racial identity, as was noted by one of her sons' identifying as white:

> **Rosie (bfp 65)** – I don't know that we ever discussed race. I think the discussion about race came up when the children began school because you have to check red, yellow or green. We told them that you are part Black and part Chinese. They could see that mom and dad had different features. We didn't make a big deal about it. If I was filling it out and there was nothing that satisfied me, I would write it in myself. When they got older, I told them they could decide if they wanted to put Afro-American or Chinese or other and write it in. I think there was some confusion. Our middle son, David, at one point thought he was white, and we had to have a discussion about that.

The first part of this quote captured a moment where Rosie spoke of racial categories on school forms and used the color "green" as a skin color. The use of this color denotes an overall discomfort towards reporting her children's race. Therefore, "green" then came to symbolize the alien quality of being multiracial to her. The end of this quote demonstrated how race was a social construct rather than an assumed, biological category. Rosie and Ted believed that their sons would "figure it out for themselves," but found themselves correcting their son when he made an inappropriate choice by identifying as white. Given his highly educated parents and their acknowledgement that they generally lived in all white neighborhoods, their son probably had every claim on an internal white racial identity, but when social push comes to social shove, racial categories were recreated and reinforced even by well-meaning, highly educated, interracially married parents.

In the end, Melvin and Alexandria seemed to be able to live lives that were affected by race to only a small degree by any measure. Race was never a main point in their lives and the lives of the people around them, while Rosie and Ted lived lives that were highly racialized and constantly under surveillance. Although Melvin and Alexandria's experiences seem to coincide with an assimilationist framework, it is clear that Rosie and Ted were together in spite of assimilation processes, rather than because of them.

Establishing a Foreign-born Asian Female/Military American Male Context

Although some issues exist that seem to rise specifically in an overseas context, the existence of the white/black paradigm, with black being considered far inferior to white, was expressed in a consistent fashion throughout my interviews with the four couples that fit the foreign-born Asian female/military American male context. This was demonstrated with the need for interracial Japanese and black couples to have to "sneak around," and with how their children were treated by extended family.

On Sneaking and Not Sneaking Around

One of the topics to come up in a foreign-born context was that Japanese/black interracial couples were conscious of the need to (space) "sneak" around. Miyoko makes this observation when she notices that all the places that Henry takes her to are dark:

> **Miyoko (afp 76)** – We just kept going to movies, and then I asked him, why you take me all the time to dark place. You know, I made a joke. Because finally I can speak a little bit. I can't see, I no can see. Oh, if you feel that way I will take you out to the club. See, club is too dark too. (laughs) We would joke like that. And he thought I was kidding, but no. Then he said okay, daylight I will take you. Let's go bowling. Bowling? Our place is so country that I didn't know what bowling looked like. And I said okay, it was so fun. And that's all. That's it.

Although it seems like Henry initiated the sneaking around behavior in this relationship, for Masako and Chris, it was all Masako's idea:

> **Masako (afp 68)** – And so we started to go to the movies, but I would never see the first or the last part because I would have to sneak in, because you never know who is watching. Because my father was born and raised in Sasabo and so he had a lot of friends, so if we go together then my father's friends would see. So he would go in first and I would go in later, and he would stand up so I could see him. And once I started watching the movie I would pay attention to the time because I have to go home, because if I was late, my father would be mad. I was 20 years old already, but my father was so strict. And so to get home in time I would have to leave about 30 minutes early, and so that is why I never saw the first part and last part of a movie. (laughs) At the time, I was going to cooking school, and I would stop by

my friend's house to get the recipe and then sneak out and go to the movies.

I followed up by asking if her father would really kill her, and then she clarified and said that he would beat her up; however, she was already past 22 years old.

> **Masako (afp 68)** – He would beat me up. He doesn't drink, but you know fathers and their daughters. My sister and I asked my father if we could go to a coffee shop and he said that he would take us. Now who wants to go with their daddy? I was already 21-22. That was how strict he was.

Although sneaking around does not seem like it is connected to race, Miyoko and Masako make it very clear that other Japanese people had a problem with their future husbands being black:

> **Miyoko (afp 76)** – Oh yeah, that's what they say, he's black! They said, no good. And I asked, why no good? And they didn't say nothing. They just said black, he's black. I said, even white? And they said, no good, because they heard about other people.

> **Masako (afp 68)** – My sister was married to a white guy and I was with Chris, and she was like, why you go with them? Especially you, why did you go with him? I said why, because he is black? I don't care about that color stuff, I love him and want to be married to him, and my mother was so mad.

So, even though the participants did not connect their sneaking around to racism and the race of their spouses, it seems clear that race was at least part of their rationale. Also, what points in the direction of racial consideration is the fact that none of the Asian women married to white American GIs spoke about sneaking around or the perceived need to sneak around.

That Oriental Stuff ...

One of the major tenets of the assimilation paradigm is that the increase of interracial marriages means that the racial barriers that existed between those two races have lessened, and that eventually these races will blend together in a manner reminiscent of the way that white ethnics do today (Waters 1990). If true, interracial marriage eventually should lead to the existence of less racialized lives for multiracial children, and ultimately, lead to a melting pot society. However, what would it mean if people of different races got together *because* of the stereotypes of the racial groups in question, rather than the fading away of these concepts?

In the case of James, white American male, and Jasmine, Filipino female, what was considered "love at first sight" for James was remembered very differently by Jasmine:

> **James (wmp 55)** – Well, my buddy and I were at a local bar after we got into port, and that is when I saw her. She was a waitress and I tell you she was something else. And so I go up and talked to her, and the rest, as they say, is history. (laughs) It was pretty much love at first sight.

> **Jasmine (afp 45)** – I was at work and I see this man walking up to me. He was handsome in his uniform. (laughs) But when he starts talking to me, he asked me how much? He thought I was a prostitute! And I told him, I am not a prostitute, you know? I am a good girl, not a prostitute.

In order for anyone to consider propositioning a woman and assuming she is a prostitute and "love at first sight" to be on the same level, one must reconcile the idea that James did what was socially normative for him to do (Enloe 2000). So, even though it may have been the norm for an American GI to approach a Filipino woman in such a manner, issues of power and status quickly come to the surface as one asks the question, would James have used the phrase "love at first sight" in connection to a prostitute of his same race? Or maybe the difference in power between the two is what sparked the relationship for him in the first place? Did he see this Asian woman as something to be possessed? And did he equate this possession to loving her?

Although the power relationship between James and Jasmine falls along racial lines, the fetishizing of Asian women comes across far more clearly with Misa and Ben. For Misa, what attracted her to him was the notion that he did not judge her based on her looks:

> **Misa (afp 57)** – He didn't care that I wore thick glasses. That increased my attraction to him, because he did not judge me on how I looked. I don't know what he sees in me. When I met him I was wearing very thick glasses, but that did not matter to him. That was very refreshing to me.

Although her physical beauty may not have played that strong of a role in Ben's attraction to Misa, it is clear that her being Asian was paramount in his decision making regarding selecting a wife:

> **Ben (wmp 56)** – It was all that Oriental stuff, man. I just love that Oriental stuff, the culture, the land, the mystique, the look. It was just for me. From the moment I met her, it was a done deal. It was just a matter of time before I convinced her. (laughs).

Ben's response strongly suggests that the woman was not as important as her race.

Even Misa, who was a college student at the time she met Ben, acknowledged that she was socially reduced to being thought of as a prostitute because of her involvement with Ben, an American GI:

> **Misa (afp 57)** – Well, my family was against it, because it was a shameful thing that I did. Because not only was he a different race, but he was a service man, and so I stooped to the level of a prostitute. That is what most people think. My good friends even thought I was doing something wrong to my parents.

Misa even states that if Ben were a foreign exchange student, their relationship would be seen very differently because Ben would be assumed to be of a higher class:

> **Misa (afp 57)** – If Ben were a transfer student and came to Japan it would be a different story. They see them as a higher social status.
>
> **Interviewer** – So, did you ever see that?
>
> **Misa (afp 57)** – No, I just know that.

But if this is the case, then this begs the question of why any foreign-born Asian women would marry an American GI in the first place?

Misa observed the pattern of very beautiful Japanese women marrying average or not so good-looking men, and suggests that "freedom" from Japanese cultural norms on women is the answer:

> **Misa (afp 57)** – You know what; I think it is the freedom that they are looking for. They can do so much more in the U.S. Myself, it just happened to be my husband. Back then I was longing for a Japanese life, but I just happened to fall in love with my husband. Back in the day, it was for financial reasons, but

> nowadays, it is an easy way to get married and get free because United States' life was more free. I think that is part of the attraction. Because I see many pretty Japanese women married to a military man, and I think, she can do better than that. (laughs).

This suggests that women who want to be "free" will make the rational choice to marry an American, and brave a whole new world and all the positive and negative aspects of it, because of looser cultural constraints for women in the U.S.

Although the United States may have looser constraints on women relative to Japan, it seems that these cultural restraints were ultimately replaced by much tighter racial constraints on Asian womanhood. These racial constraints ranged from being considered a prostitute, being submissive and being the servants of Americans:

> **Misa (afp 57)** – Oh yes, most of the military wives think that we are nothing but prostitutes, even though many of us were not. They think that we are uneducated. But they didn't know that I already had my AA degree in Japan because I went to junior college. They tried to take advantage of us, because they thought we were very submissive. So they thought they could do whatever they want to do, they would ask us to do certain things.

> **Miyoko (afp 76)** – One time, at a working place, he said she was nice. And I said, okay, do you wanna come to my house? And she said okay. And so this lady brings two friends, they never came to my house before. And she brings a whole bunch of laundry to wash. Then she asked, do you mind if I wash my clothes in your washing machine? And I said, okay, go ahead. That's funny. It's the first day, and I don't even know her.

In other words, it seems that the looser cultural norms were more closely related to American women, not foreign-born Asian women.

So although the assimilationist paradigm would suggest that the barriers between the races would need to be broken down before substantial interracial marriage could occur, this analysis suggests that racial stereotypes and power norms do not need to be eliminated in order to interracially marry. On the contrary, it could be hypothesized that substantial interracial marriage happens *because* of racial stereotypes, rather than their lack of existence.

The Difference Between White and Black Mixed Children

It is clear from the respondents in my research that Japanese people do not like interracial couples; however, it is also clear that whiteness was a privileged category. Although both were bad, it was clear that being married to a white person was considered better than being married to someone black:

> **Misa (afp 57)** – In her case, she is in a worse position than I am in the U.S., because she wants to be friends to Japanese ladies, but they look down on her because her husband is black.

So if this is the case, a natural question that would follow from this space would be to ask does white privilege extend towards the children?

When asked about taking her children back to Japan to live, Misa states that she would not do that because even though they are mixed with white, they would be treated poorly because they are not pure Japanese:

> **Misa (afp 57)** – Yes, because they are mixed race. It doesn't matter who is the daddy or the mommy, your chances are not as good as pure Japanese. I am going to keep my kids over here. I am not going to take them back.

She speaks directly to this lack of acceptance by Japanese children when she reflected on a time where they lived in Japan and had to enroll her children in a Japanese school:

> **Misa (afp 57)** – Nowadays, most young Japanese don't care, but they still make some comments. Like when we went home in '86, my kids enrolled in Japanese school, because my neighbor worked in city hall and he helped us. Once my kids went to the pool, the kids thought since they were different that they did not need a swimming cap. So the kids would make comments. They were nice, because they never saw Japanese kids that did not speak English. So for that, they were nice. But they were only nice on the outside, deep in it was not there.

Although serious, the extent of these infractions does not suggest that her children would not ultimately be accepted by Japanese people. This hypothesis is further supported by how Misa's brother disowned her because of her interracial marriage, but loved his niece and nephew:

> **Misa (afp 57)** – But the person that was against it the most was my brother.
>
> **Interviewer** – What did he say?
>
> **Misa (afp 57)** – You are going to get married and have children with that red-haired son-of-a-bitch? Then he didn't talk to me for close to 20 years. He did not talk to me until my father's funeral. That was when he started to talk to me. He talked to my husband, the guy that he called such a bad name, when I went to Japan. My brother would try to speak English to him, and he loved my two kids, especially my daughter. He spoiled her rotten. He didn't talk to me, but he was very good with my kids.

The negative association with being mixed with black was established when talking with Masako about how she was told that she could not come back home because her children were black:

> **Masako (afp 68)** – Later on I found out I was pregnant and Chris had to leave, but my father said that I could stay home until the baby was born, but you will not bring that baby into my house. Chris had to go to the Vietnam War, but I could not stay with my father because he said I can't bring my black baby in the house. So then I thought, I will go with Chris to the United States with his family. Although I would not know anybody, I could not stay with my parents after my father said that I cannot stay with them after my baby is born.

Although Masako and her father reconciled, the privileging of whiteness is clearly established in the manner that he treated his grandchildren. Masako's sister also interracially married, but with a white American GI, and that is when Masako noticed the difference in how her father treated her mixed black children versus her sister's mixed white children:

> **Masako (afp 68)** – At the time my parents had a coffee shop, and when their friends came over my father said, take the kids upstairs, because they did not want their friends to see them. But my sister was home at the same time, but it was okay because they were white kids. And so my parents would take the grandkids to different places, so only once my parents took my children to the beach. I know that my parents loved their grandkids, but my father stayed in a small town, and everyone knew my father, and so I guess he felt ashamed that they are black.

So, even though her parents supposedly loved their grandchildren, it is clear that their mixed black grandchildren were a source of shame, while their mixed white grandchildren were a source of pride. Therefore, white privilege again comes to the forefront within the context of how the children were treated by their relatives.

"It's Just Different": Interracial Marriages and the Reformation of the Color Line

Moving from an interracially married parent's perspective to the lived experiences of Asian/white and Asian/black people is necessary to try and determine if their lives support an assimilationist framework or not. Although interethnic marriages between European ethnicities may symbolize the breakdown of ethnic barriers for people who consider themselves white (Waters 1990), I argue that the experiences of Asian/white and Asian/black children with their interracial families do not support this notion. As will be clearly demonstrated within parental advisement regarding dating practices, the parents of multiracial children maintained racist notions regarding the superiority of whiteness, especially when speaking of black suitability as marriage partners.

Within an Asian/White Context

When speaking about dating, Lenny stated clearly that he had dated women of every race:

> **Lenny (awm 22)** – No, it did not affect it. I have been with every race, you name it, Black, White, Mexican, Chinese and etc., you name it. It's not fun dancing with White girls. Even when we would go out to the club in the Navy, it was kind of reverse, all the Black dudes knew how to dance. I was one of the few, other than the Blacks, that knew how to dance. So when I would be dancing, they would say, look at him.

Although people of all races were accepted by Lenny, his Filipina mother clearly stated that she wanted him and his siblings to date white people:

> **Lenny (awm 22)** – I wouldn't, my mom would. Yes, she really wanted me to date White girls ... I would ask her, why do you want me to date just White girls, she didn't even want me to date Filipino girls. I don't know where that comes from. My sister

and I would ask where does that come from, why does she always want us to date White people? I remember dating a Black girl and telling her, and she would say rude things. I would say, why are you saying things like that? I would call it old thinking. When I would bring home a Filipino, she was still not happy. Every time I bring home a White girl, it was fine.

The privileging of whiteness by his mother may have been the result of an internalization of the superiority of whiteness through the Spanish and U.S. colonial periods of the Philippines (Ngozi-Brown 1997).

In trying to justify his mother's actions as not racist, Lenny actually reinforced the concept that white people had an assumed higher wealth status than all other races, but they are especially higher in status than black people:

Lenny (awm 22) – I think my mom wants me to date a White girl because White people are well-established and my mom's whole thing is money. I don't know why she always wanted me to date White girls, but most White people generally always have more money than say a Black person or a Filipino person would.

Although this argument was couched as a difference in class, white supremacy revealed itself in the assumption that white people are more suitable as marriage partners as a race, with no regard for each person as an individual.

If this was not clear enough, Leonard's parents actually had a family discussion on the matter of his white father cleaning up his Filipina mother's bloodline:

Leonard (awm 35) – Yeah, I remember one specific incidence with my father, the light person in the family, told us in front of our mother that you should all marry white people because I started cleaning up your mother's bloodline. And my mother agreed.

This discussion was in direct response to the dating practices of Leonard and his siblings, who did not seem to appreciate the fact that they were supposed to follow their mother's example and marry someone lighter:

Leonard (awm 35) – And, uh, it was one of those, you know, we're teenagers, we're starting to date. You know, and my dad was upset. They knew that we had boyfriends who were of color, or who really were Filipino looking, you know? And we're like, you know, we could pass, depending on what group we are in, we could pass for whatever group we're in. Um, and he sat us down. We were just talking, it was on vacation. I really cleaned up your mother's bloodline.

Although his parents had this discussion with their children regarding who they should marry, it did not seem to work as well as they would have hoped, because two out of the three siblings who are married, actually married someone of a dark complexion. However, the one son who did marry a white woman has a higher status in their mother's eyes because of the whiteness of his children:

> **Leonard (awm 35)** – And you know, I mean to this day, I mean, she would deny it, but she favors my brother who married the white skinned girl, the Italian woman. My sister married a dark skinned Samoan, my brother married a dark skinned Filipino, and she just loves those white babies better.
>
> **Interviewer** – Really?
>
> **Leonard (awm 35)** – I mean it is obvious. She would never say it, you know, but there is some kind of celebrity-hood they have because of their pigment.

When asked how the privileging of whiteness came about with his Filipina mother, Leonard suggests that it is because of colonization by various different races of people that is at the heart of it:

> **Leonard (awm 35)** – I think, Filipinos in particular, because of the history of colonization blasé, blasé, very, very, admirable, admiring whiteness. My parents were vested in my whiteness ... It might be extreme, but I don't think it is out of character for Filipino families to admire whiteness.

Although this may be a large part of the answer within a Filipino context, this would not be able to adequately explain white privilege within a Japanese context as the following cases demonstrate.

Although Lenny's and Leonard's parents seemed only to view things as either white or not white, James' white mother definitely set up the framework that white was superior to black, while Asian was somewhere in the middle. This was uncovered in a discussion that James had with his mother about who he should marry:

> **James (awm 22)** – Well, you know your family the best. It was like she was saying you'd better get an "A" on that test, or "B." A

"B" is still passing, it's not what I want, but it's acceptable. She better be white, (lowers his voice) or Asian, that's acceptable. Maybe she sees me like my dad and thinks that I should have a woman like her, I don't know.

This construction made it clear that white was an "A," while Asian was a "B." However, black was clearly an "F" as uncovered by James as he tried to joke with his mother by having a friend, who was a black woman, act like his girlfriend:

James (awm 22) – I have a friend that's black, and she and I just played one time, and that was not cool. I'm not friends with her anymore because of that. My mom and my grandfather acted really stupid. I couldn't believe that they would be such assholes. So I started with me telling my mom that I was in love with this girl, and she said, yeah right. Then she said, you better be joking! And my friend was fine with it until my mom said, you better be joking. Then my grandfather said, do you want to take care of someone who's lazy for the rest of your life? And then he said, no offense, I'm sure you're not, but the rest of you are. What do you say about that? She was cool, she was educated and she was from France, actually.

As one can note from the comments of the white grandfather, James' mother did not fall very far from the tree. However, what became an issue for me was to wonder why James would subject his friend, whose friendship he lost as a result of this "joke," to the possibility of such racist behavior? Did his mother's notions of white supremacy enter into this space where he made a "friend" into a "test subject"?

When confronted by James about his mother's racist beliefs, she embedded her concerns regarding him marrying a black woman within the context of worrying about what the children would be:

James (awm 22) – My mom would say if I got married to a black woman, then what would the kids be? Well, they would be Asian, black and white, whatever I am. I don't know why that's such a big deal, it's not the 60s, 70s or 30s. It still happens today, but is not nearly as bad as it was back then. She would say, think about your kids, they're not going to know what they are. Then how in the hell was I supposed to know what I was? She would say, you would choose, you are both, you were raised both. Then she said, it's just different.

James stated that if he were to marry a black woman, then his children would be black, Asian and white, but the assertion of his mother that being married to a black person was "different" strongly suggests that his mother understood the concept of the "one drop rule" on an intuitive level, if not a conscious level (Frankenberg 1993; Nagashima 1992). In other words, the proper response in this framework was that people who are of Asian/white backgrounds can choose their racial identity, while if you were mixed with black, society would choose your identity for you, and that would be black (Davis 1991).

Although James' mother seemed particularly concerned with the racial categorization of hypothetical grandchildren, this concern did not seem to extend itself to the character of the women that her sons were involved with:

> **James (awm 22)** – She would say this behind closed doors, but she's never open with it. If someone would ask her she would say it is my decision, she just wants someone who will make me happy. And I'm like, bullshit, you just told me something completely different than that. Now don't get me wrong, I love my mom, but one of her jobs is to make sure that her sons marry the right girl. My brother has a fiancée, who is very rude, but my parents accept her. I guarantee you if she was any other race, she would have been gone a long time ago. Rude, ungrateful, self-centered, egotistical, I could keep going. But she fits into what my mom wanted.

This was a direct case where white privilege acted as a shield to overall bad behavior. This was duly noted when James made the observation that if his potential sister-in-law were a woman of any other race, his mother would have had issues with her, but since she was white, she was all right.

In the end, James seemingly alleviated his parents' concerns regarding his potential marriage partner by being involved with a woman who was of Filipina and white background:

> **James (awm 22)** – My dad was cool, but I know that when I got the girlfriend that I have now that it was a relief, because she's Filipino and white ... So it's good that I have a white Asian girlfriend, because that's about as good as my mom and dad could get. They keep saying it's just the kids and the social class you give in an interracial marriage.

This construction maintains racial categories and adds another racial category for consideration: being multiracial (Hollinger 1995). However, now people who are multiracial need to stay within the new multiracial category for a potential spouse.

The importance of a white/black continuum continued with Karen, as her Asian father and grandparents firmly established the black/white dichotomy within her dating practices:

> **Karen (awf 18)** – I was dating a Black guy, and I brought him to the house to meet my parents. When my grandma found out about it, I had to go to her house. She basically yelled at me and told me I had to stop dating him. I told her that it was my life and I was going to do what I wanted. I told her that she didn't stop my mom from marrying my dad, but she said that was different. She didn't like him because he was Black ... She thought the guy I was with was lazy before she even met him.

Not only did her grandmother yell at her, but her Asian father also was angry with her for dating a black man:

> **Karen (awf 18)** – My dad was furious, and his beliefs are the same as my grandmother's. My mom was upset because she thought no one should tell me what I should do with my life. She's been like that with my grandma. My grandmother feels like if I'm involved with someone who isn't Japanese, I'm ruining the bloodline. My dad thinks that too, but he won't say it to your face.

This quote encapsulated notions of white being constructed as pure, or at the very least neutral, while black was seen as a pollutant to the family bloodline. Karen's grandmother clearly stated that being involved with anyone not Japanese would dilute the bloodline, but allowed her son to marry a white woman. This strongly suggested that Karen's Japanese grandparents actually saw themselves as white. Although this seems to fly in the face of U.S. racial categorization, this notion can be partially substantiated by Lopez, where Japanese people made the legal claim that they should be considered white (Lopez 1996).

Karen picked up on the seemingly contradictory comparisons between black and white and confronted her father about it:

> **Karen (awf 18)** – That is my biggest issue, because I ask him what the difference is. I ask him if I marry either a Black guy or a White guy, would he disown me? They're both not Japanese. He said as long as they are disciplined and supportive, it didn't matter. Then I ask him, why we stop then after I tell you he's Black? I tell him that the guy is in college and working towards his bachelor's degree, but he only hears one thing. He says I can't talk to him like that because he's the head of the house. Later, I did find some stuff out about the guy, and my dad threw it in my

face. My dad still tries to talk to me about Japanese guys to get the ball rolling again. It's hard because I'm eighteen, and I have my whole life ahead of me. My dad wants my children to have Japanese names, and I do too because being Japanese is something I'm very proud of and don't want to lose it. I don't want to lose that; it's a touchy subject.

Karen did not challenge her father's racial lumping practices, which made all black men like the one she was dating, but this probably had to do with her being so young, and the Japanese cultural attribute of strict obedience towards authority (Schneider and Silverman 2003; Smythe 1953). Karen further admitted to the fact that, although she was looking for more serious relationships, she clearly felt limited in her options, even with other Asian ethnicities:

Karen (awf 18) – It is more about what my dad thinks even before my grandmother's whole deal. Right now, I am looking for something more serious, and I don't want to do things anymore. I am focusing on what is going to be serious. I do want someone who has Japanese traits to preserve that. I want to keep my options open, but I think about how it would never work out because he's White or Afro-American or Mexican. I haven't dated everyone in the rainbow, but my dad hasn't been pleased with any of them. I think any father would be leery of any guy dating his daughter. I remember one time I did bring home an Asian guy, and he was so happy and excited. When my dad found out he was Vietnamese, the doors shut again ... He called him a "gook," and that he's not good enough for me. Even though he was Asian, he still wasn't good.

This demonstrates that Karen's father believed that all other Asian ethnicities were inferior to the Japanese, which is strongly supported in research about the socially constructed superiority of the Japanese to all other Asians (Kowner 2000; Morris-Suzuki 1998; Smythe and Naitoh 1953).

These experiences actually follow an assimilationist framework, as people of Asian heritage fight to improve their social placement in the racial hierarchy by intermarrying with white Americans, while willfully not marrying black Americans.

Within an Asian/Black Context

Although Asian and white parents externally enforced the black/white paradigm because they told their children not to marry someone who was black, Jane's black father was an example of how white supremacy notions of racial hierarchy were enforced internally. This internal enforcement was noted by Jane who was dating a Chinese man at the time of her father's confrontation with him:

> **Jane (abf 24)** – One time my father confronted my Chinese boyfriend. My boyfriend called my house, and my father answered the phone and asked him where he lived. My boyfriend got freaked out because my dad was asking him 20 questions, so he lied to my dad about where he lived. He gave him a street, but he said he didn't know his house number, which is stupid because you have to know where you live. (laughs) So my dad said that he didn't like liars and that he didn't want liars to be hanging out with his daughter, so my father told him not to come around the house again. Being a teenager, of course I thought it was the end of the world, and this is where my father and I parted ways; but other than my boyfriend being a liar, my father broke it down for me and said, your boyfriend is Chinese and that his family is never going to accept you and that I needed to understand that. And I said, just because you have problems with mom's family doesn't mean I will. Things are different now. And I remember that he gave me a hug and said someday I would understand, and I pushed him away and said, I hate you. I thought that was one of the most hurtful things you can hear coming from your parents, that you have to choose who you date because their family is not going to accept you.

Although most would say that he was only being a concerned father, by suggesting that his daughter would someday understand his concerns strongly suggested that he too has assumed that black people were unsuitable mates to people who are not black. This concept was further established by a discussion with her aunts that questioned the availability of black men in California:

> **Jane (abf 24)** – Oh, here's another story, I was visiting my aunts in New Jersey and I was calling my boyfriend, and they asked me, who is this boy that I'm calling? They asked me, what is he, and I told them he's Asian, then they asked, don't they have any black guys in California? I told them, yes, there are black men in California, and they told me I should bring a nice black boy home. And they tell me that I should move to New Jersey and find a nice black man.

Although this quote did not set up the color line in the same manner that it has with Asian and white people, one must ask the question as to whether black people can accept and use notions of racial categorization, and also not internalize the racial hierarchy that *must* come with it.

This question was answered by Jane herself, as she told of a story that involved her Chinese boyfriend who was a bodyboarder:

> **Jane (abf 24)** – Also, one more story, I dated a Chinese guy who was a bodyboarder, this is one of the things I'm embarrassed about. We would be at the beach and it would be hot, and I would be the only moron sitting there with pants and a hooded sweatshirt with my hood on. And the dumb part of it was that he asked me to wear his sweater so that I wouldn't get dark, and I did. And I hate myself for that, and when I look back and think how non self-respecting can you be? That someone can tell you what skin tone you can have or not have. So, I've come a long way. (laughs).

This quote made it clear that it was possible for people of Asian/black backgrounds to internalize black inferiority, while at the same time giving hope for the future of race relations through her current assertion of pride in who she is as a person. Again, the experiences of people of Asian/black backgrounds do not fit into an assimilationist framework, as it is clearly demonstrated that part of being American is knowing where you are at on the racial hierarchy, and that the bottom of that hierarchy is blackness.

Conclusion

In conclusion, although interracial marriages have been heralded as the end point of the assimilation process and would usher in a period where racial categories and racial hierarchy would be ended, this is clearly not the case in my sample. Starting with the experiences of an Asian and white couple and comparing them to an Asian and black couple, where the man was Asian in both cases, revealed startling differences regarding the assimilation process that lay directly along racial lines. Being married to either a white or a black person was woven into every experience, from how the couples met to dating practices and child rearing, which all privileged whiteness.

Interracial marriages between the Asian and white people in my sample consistently reinforced racial hierarchy upon their children, which was seen most clearly with dating practices. The distinction was explicitly stated that being married to someone who was black was different, and this difference was linked to the social construction of black at the bottom of the racial hierarchy.

Assimilation processes seemed to be working, if only partially, in the cases of Asian and white interracial couples and people of Asian/white backgrounds in my sample, as they assimilated towards Anglo conformity. Being of Asian/white backgrounds did allow more choices that regarded racial identity within an interracial Asian and white family, but these same choices were not afforded to their children outside of a white/black framework. What was also noted in the experiences of Jane and her family was that the notion of black inferiority could be internalized by black people themselves, and this was evident through the family's limiting of Jane's dating practices, and because the rejection of black people as acceptable mates was assumed and internalized.

Notes

1. wfp = white female parent
2. bfp = black female parent
3. amp = Asian male parent
4. afp = Asian female parent

6
Conclusion

In conclusion, what my research has clearly demonstrated is that equating race to ethnicity has led the multiracial project to wrongly promote that an increase in the number of people of Asian/white and Asian/black backgrounds and the increase in interracial marriages with Asians signifies the end of racial categories and the completion of the assimilation process for all racial groups. The idea that people of Asian/white and Asian/black backgrounds will challenge racial categories was roundly refuted, as it was found that the multiracial people in my sample used biological notions of race to construct their racial identities, which made the distinctions between racial categories more rigid and essentialist, rather than less. Therefore, after interviewing thirty-two people of Asian/white and Asian/black backgrounds and six pairs of interracial Asian and white and Asian and black parents, what can be concluded is that racial meanings have become *stronger* and that the lines between racial categories have become *clearer*, due largely to the current multiracial project.

Although the people of Asian/white and Asian/black backgrounds in my sample fought against constrained notions of their racial identities, their experiences with society demonstrated the continued salience of a white/black color line in the United States and in Asian countries. Although many people of Asian/white backgrounds in my sample developed a white identity, whether rational or constrained, the overall effect served to grant privileges and lessen discrimination by Asian and white people.

However, this was not the case for people of Asian/black backgrounds in my sample, as they were treated as "just black" by people of Asian and white backgrounds, both in the United States and in Asian countries, and suffered through many racist experiences ranging from name calling to on the job discrimination to physical abuse. However, the Asian/black people in my sample were also treated as a marginalized other by other black people, especially in the case of black women towards Asian/black women.

Assimilationist notions of the meaning of the increase of interracial families were put into serious question, as it was clearly demonstrated that the interracial couples in my study could still be racist towards black people, and even people of their own racial groups. Interracially married Asian and white couples were accepted, although not really appreciated, by family and peer groups, while the Asian and black couples in my sample were often disowned by immediate family members. Furthermore, interracially married Asian and white couples in my study reestablished and reaffirmed white supremacy notions of black unsuitability as marriage partners time and time again to their children when they had chosen to date someone who was black.

Understanding the inherent hierarchy of racial categories suggests that there can never be a true cultural pluralism model within the U.S. because this paradigm assumes that races can be considered equal, but my research strongly implies that they cannot. This inequality, coupled with the "one drop rule," also strongly suggests that a true melting pot model cannot exist because blackness is something that will never *melt* away. However, there is some evidence that the people of Asian/white backgrounds in my sample are moving towards an Anglo conformity identity, since some rationally chose or were socially constrained to do so. What this suggests is that there could be a radical reordering of who is considered white in the United States, which will include people of Asian/white backgrounds as white, while reestablishing the inferiority of blackness (Yancey 2003; Davis 1991).

Ultimately, this research has uncovered that the concepts of race and assimilation are inherently incompatible, and that the multiracial project in its current construction is being used to reify and quantify racial categories (R. Spencer 2011). Racial hegemony is keeping pace with the challenges that people of Asian/white and Asian/black backgrounds are supposed to present by allowing racial groups themselves to develop, create and enforce their identities, thus continuing to push people who claim multiple racial backgrounds to the margins, while constantly redeveloping, recreating and reinforcing white supremacy.

Data notwithstanding, this conclusion does not mean that I do not believe that people of multiracial backgrounds could not be used to challenge and eventually end the concepts of race and racism. In order to do this, first, multiracial people must create a racial project that focuses on racial justice first, and racial identity second. Second, people of multiracial backgrounds need to help academia, by doing research themselves or being research subjects, continue to develop a clear understanding of how race is a social construction, but has very real consequences, by using their lived lives as an example of how race is constantly shifting and fluctuating, and yet still maintains white supremacy. Third, multiracial people themselves must refuse to use biological notions of race to explain their attitudes, aptitudes and abilities and not allow other people, including their own families and friends, to do so. And fourth, multiracial people must not further (re)enforce white supremacy by taking race into consideration specifically regarding the suitability of black people as marriage partners, and teach this to their children.

The steps that I just proposed would be the *beginning*, not the *end*, of what the current multiracial project must change in order to come closer to being the vehicle against race and racism that it is proposed to be. However, what is apparent through my research is that a multiracial project that does not have a clear and purposeful ideology that is centered on anti-racist beliefs and the social construction of race will only serve to reimagine how we think of race, while still maintaining the centrality and supremacy of whiteness.

Appendix A
How the Sample was Generated

Respondents were recruited through snowball sampling. I first used personal networks of multiracial people and interracial families with adult aged children to generate the first round of interviews. I then asked these respondents for additional references, including, but not limited to, siblings and personal associates. This technique eliminated the possibility of a random sample; therefore, this study will only be used to draw information that would allow for the creation of a meaningful theoretical model that may later lead to more positivistic results.

Snowball sampling was necessary because of several difficulties that complicate finding people of multiracial backgrounds without the use of personal networks. First, the number of people of diverse racial backgrounds was relatively small (2.4 percent of the U.S. population, according to the 2000 Census); therefore, efforts to conduct research regarding this group required a more direct recruiting approach (Williams 1996).

Second, personal knowledge of a person's diverse racial backgrounds was necessary, because many mixed-race people do not "look" different, and/or do not have any physically distinguishing characteristics that differentiate them from any particular mono-racial group. This observation was important, because any theoretical model that attempted to understand how people of multiracial backgrounds experience race must include those persons who were multiracial but may have been racially ambiguous or completely like one particular race. Therefore, this project did not randomly approach people who *looked* multiracial in public spaces. Even though it was possible to generate a sample in this manner, this method would have eliminated the people of diverse racial backgrounds who had a phenotype that would not differentiate them from other mono-racial groups.

Third, many people of multiracial backgrounds may not have responded to ads in newspapers or newsletters requesting multiracial subjects, because they did not personally identify as being multiracial

(Hall 1992; William 1996; Thornton and Gates 2001). This reasoning was further supported, and complicated, by research that convincingly demonstrated that people of diverse racial backgrounds have answered ads that requested mono-racial participants (Cauce et al. 1992).

And fourth, but related to ad placement, was the question of which newspapers should a researcher place ads in, asking for multiracial participants? The researchers who have used ads to recruit multiracial Asian/Black subjects have placed them in the local newspaper, but also in the local Asian American newspaper (Hall 1992), and websites specializing in multiracial identity (Hall and Turner 2001). This approach, however, may have oversampled people of diverse racial backgrounds that identified as multiracial, and again, may not have adequately represented those that categorize themselves mono-racially.

Appendix B
Interview Questions for Multiracial Persons

Pseudonym: _____
Sex: _____ **Age:** _____ **Height:** _____
Birthplace: _____
Mother's race: _____ **Birthplace (country):** _____
Father's race: _____ **Birthplace (country):** _____
*If parents are from different countries:
Did you ever visit your mother's homeland? _____ Father's? _____
Did you ever live in your mother's homeland? _____ Father's? _____
If yes, approximately how many years? _____ Father's? _____
Did you ever live in Hawaii? _____
Were either of your parents in the U.S. military? _____ Which one? _____ What branch? _____ Officer or enlisted? _____
Eye color: _____ Hair Color: _____ Hair Texture: _____

1) How do you identify yourself racially? Explain.
2) On a scale of 1 to 5, with 1 being none and 5 being completely, how _____ do you believe you look?

0	1	2	3	4	5
Don't Know	None	Slightly	Moderately	Very	Completely

3) On a scale of 1 to 5, with 1 being none and 5 being completely, how _____ do you believe others think you look?

0	1	2	3	4	5
Don't Know	None	Slightly	Moderately	Very	Completely

4) On a scale of 1 to 5, with 1 being none and 5 being completely identify, how closely do you personally identify with being _____?

0	1	2	3	4	5
Don't Know	None	Slightly	Moderately	Very	Completely

5) On a scale of 1 to 5, with 1 being complete rejection and 5 being complete acceptance, to what degree do you believe that _____ people accept you as being?

0	1	2	3	4	5
Don't Know	Complete Rejection	Mostly Reject	Some of Both	Mostly Accept	Complete Acceptance

6) On a scale of 1 to 5, with 1 being none and 5 being completely, how _____ do you believe you look?

0	1	2	3	4	5
Don't Know	None	Slightly	Moderately	Very	Completely

7) On a scale of 1 to 5, with 1 being none and 5 being completely, how _____ do you believe others think you look?

0	1	2	3	4	5
Don't Know	None	Slightly	Moderately	Very	Completely

8) On a scale of 1 to 5, with 1 being none and 5 being completely identify, how closely do you personally identify with being _____?

0	1	2	3	4	5
Don't Know	None	Slightly	Moderately	Very	Completely

9) On a scale of 1 to 5, with 1 being complete rejection and 5 being complete acceptance, to what degree do you believe that _____ people accept you as being?

0	1	2	3	4	5
Don't Know	Complete Rejection	Mostly Reject	Some of Both	Mostly Accept	Complete Acceptance

10) Did you have any experiences that you feel are related to your racial heritage while you were growing up? If so, please explain.
11) Are there any other racial/ethnic communities that you have interacted with that you feel accept or reject you? Explain.
12) What about other types of groups, e.g., athletic teams, cheerleading, speech and debate or drama club?
13) Some families talk to their children about race and some don't. Tell me how race was discussed by your folks?
14) Is there anything that you would like to add to this interview that you thought we were going to talk about that we have not covered?

Appendix C
Interview Questions for Interracially Married Parent

Pseudonym: _____
Birthplace: _____
Age/gender of children: _____
Age: _____ **Race:** _____ **Spouse's race:** _____

1) Please tell me about the day you and your spouse met.
2) How did the people in your life, e.g., your parents, siblings and friends, feel about you dating someone of a different race?
3) Did you have any experiences that you believe are related to your interracial marriage? If so, please explain.
4) On a scale of 1 to 5, with 1 being complete rejection and 5 being complete acceptance, to what degree do you believe that _____ people accept your marriage?

0	1	2	3	4	5
Don't Know	Complete Rejection	Mostly Reject	Some of Both	Mostly Accept	Complete Acceptance

5) On a scale of 1 to 5, with 1 being complete rejection and 5 being complete acceptance, to what degree do you believe that _____ people accept your interracial marriage?

0	1	2	3	4	5
Don't Know	Complete Rejection	Mostly Reject	Some of Both	Mostly Accept	Complete Acceptance

6) Some families talk to their children about race and some don't. Tell me how race was discussed in your household?

7) Is there anything that you would like to add to this interview that you thought we were going to talk about that we have not covered?

Bibliography

Alexander, Sandy. 2006. "Parents Raise Awareness of Disease That Took the Child." *Knight Rider Tribune Business News*. November 29.

Allen, James P. 1997. "Recent Immigration from the Philippines and Filipino Communities in the United States." *Geographical Review* Vol. 67, No. 2: 195-208.

Allman, Karen Maeda. 1995. "(Un)Natural Boundaries: Mixed Race, Gender, and Sexuality." In *The Multiracial Experience*. 277-290.

American Friends Service Committee. http://en.wikipedia.org/wiki/American_Friends_Service_Committee.

Ashe, Bertram D. 1995. "'Why Don't He like My Hair?': Constructing African-American Standards of Beauty in Toni Morrison's Song of Solomon and Zora Neale Hurston's Their Eyes Were Watching God." *African-American review* Vol. 29, No. 4: 579-592.

Asuncion-Lande, Nobleza. 1971. "Multilingualism, Politics, and 'Filipinism.'" *Asian Survey* Vol. 11, No. 7: 677-692.

Bidney, D. 1942. "On the Philosophy of Culture in the Social Sciences." *The Journal of Philosophy* Vol. 39, No. 17: 449-457.

Borders, Florence E. 1988. "Researching Creole and Cajun Music's in New Orleans." *Black Music Research Journal* Vol. 8, No. 1: 15-31.

Boyd, Monica. 1971. "The Chinese in New York, California, and Hawaii: A Study of Socioeconomic Differentials." *Phylon* Vol. 32, No. 2: 198-206.

Bradshaw, Carla K. 1992. "Beauty and the Beast: On Racial Ambiguity." In *Racially Mixed People in America*. 77-90.

Brubaker, Rogers and Frederick Cooper. 2000. "Beyond 'Identity.'" *Theory and Society* Vol. 29, No. 1: 1-47.

Brunn, Stanley D. and James O. Wheeler. 1971. "Spatial Dimensions of Poverty in the United States." *Geografiska Annaler. Series B, Human Geography* Vol. 53, No. 1: 6-15.

Brunsma, David L. 2006. *Mixed Messages: Multiracial Identities in the "Color-Blind" Era*. Boulder: Lynne Rienner Publishers.

Brunsma, David L. 2006. "Mixed Messages: Doing Race in the Color-Blind Era." In *Mixed Messages: Multiracial Identities in the "Color-Blind" Era*. 1-14.

Burkhardt, William R. 1983. "Institutional Barriers, Marginality, and Adaption among the American Japanese Mixed Bloods in Japan." *The Journal of Asian Studies* Vol. 42, No. 3: 519-544.

Burma, John H. 1951. "The Background of the Current Situation of Filipino Americans." *Social Forces* Vol. 30, No. 1: 42-48.

Campbell, Christopher P. 1995. *Race, Myth and the News*. Thousand Oaks: Sage Publications.
Cauce, Ana Marie et al. 1992. "Between a Rock and a Hard Place: Social Adjustment of Biracial Youth." In *Racially Mixed People in America*. 207-222.
Cole, David. 2010. "No Equal Justice: Race and Class in the American Criminal Justice System." In *The Social Construction of Difference and Inequality*. 380-388.
Collins, Patricia Hill. 2000. *Black Feminist Thought*. New York: Routledge.
Comas-Diaz, Lillian. 1995. "LatiNegra: Mental Health Issues of African Latinas." In *The MultiracialExperience*. 167-190.
Comas, Juan. 1961. "'Scientific' Racism Again?" *Current Anthropology* Vol. 2, No. 4: 303-340.
Cornyetz, Nina. 1994. "Fetishized Blackness: Hip-Hop and Racial Desire in Contemporary Japan." *Social Text* 41: 113-139.
Coronado, Marc et al. 2003. *Crossing Lines: Race and Mixed Race across the Geohistorical Divide*. Santa Barbara: Multiethnic Student Outreach.
DaCosta, Kimberly McClain. 2006. "Selling Mixedness: Marketing with Multiracial Identities." In *Mixed Messages: Multiracial Identities in the "Color-Blind" Era*.
Daniel, G. Reginald. 1992. "Beyond Black and White." In *Racially Mixed People in America*. 333-341.
Daniel, G. Reginald. 1992. "Passers and Pluralists: Subverting the Racial Divide." In *Racially MixedPeople in America*. 91-107.
Davis, Angela Y. 1981. *Women, Race & Class*. New York: Vintage Books.
Davis, F. James. 1991. *Who is Black?* University Park: The Pennsylvania State University Press.
Donoghue, John D. 1957. "An Eta Community in Japan: The Social Persistence of Outcaste Groups." *American Anthropologist*, New Series, Vol. 59, No. 6: 1000-1017.
Enloe, Cynthia. 2000. *Maneuvers*. Berkeley: University of California Press.
Espiritu, Yen Le. 1992. *Asian American Panethnicity*. Philadelphia: Temple University Press.
Ewen, Stewart and Elizabeth Ewen. 1992. *Channels of Desire: Mass Images and the Shaping of American Consciousness*. Minneapolis: University Of Minnesota Press.
Feagin, Joe R. and Clairece Booher Feagin. 1999. *Racial and Ethnic Relations*. Sixth Edition. Upper Saddle River: Prentice-Hall.
Fernandez, Carlos A. 1995. "Government Classification of Multiracial/Multiethnic People." In *The Multiracial Experience*. 15-36.
Fernandez, Carlos A. 1992. "La Raza And the Melting Pot: A Comparative Look at Multiethnicity." In *Racially Mixed People in America*. 126-143.
Fine, Michael J. et al. 2005. "The Role of Race in Genetics and Health Disparities Research." *American Journal of Public Health*. Vol. 95, Iss. 12: 2125.
Fong, Hiram L. 1971. "Immigration and Naturalization Laws: Today's Need for Naturalization Law Reform." *International Migration Review* Vol. 5, No. 4, Naturalization and Citizenship: US Policies, Procedures and Problems. 406-418.

Frankenberg, Ruth. 1993. *The Social Construction of Whiteness: White Women, Race Matters.* Minneapolis: University of Minnesota Press.
Friedman, Lester D. 1991. *Unspeakable Images: Ethnicity and the American Cinema.* Urbana: University of Illinois Press.
Fulbeck, Kip. 2006. *Part Asian 100% Hapa.* San Francisco: Chronicle Books.
Furedi, Frank. 2002. "How Sociology Imagined 'Mixed Race.'" In *Rethinking 'Mixed Race.'* 23-41.
Gaskins, Pearl Fuyo. 1999. *What are You?* New York: Henry Holt and Company.
Gibbs, Jewelle Taylor and Alice M. Hines. 1992. "Negotiating Ethnic Identity: Issues for Black-White Biracial Adolescents." In *Racially Mixed People in America.* 223-238.
Gilbert, Dennis. 1998. *The American Class Structure: In an Age of Growing Inequality.* Fifth Edition. Belmont: Wadsworth Publishing Company.
Gilroy, Paul. 2000. *Against Race.* Cambridge: The Belknap Press of Harvard University.
Graham, Susan R. 1995. "Grassroots Advocacy." In *American Mixed Race.* 185-190.
Graham, Susan R. 1995. "The Real World." In *The Multiracial Experience.* 37-48.
Gordon, Milton M. 1964. *Assimilation in American Life.* New York: Oxford University Press.
Guay, Louis. 2006. "The Human Genome Diversity Project: An Ethnography of Scientific Practice." *The Canadian Review of Sociology and Anthropology* Vol. 43, Iss. 2: 236.
Guevarra, Rudy P. Jr. 2005. "Burritos and Bagoong: Mexipinos and Multiethnic Identity in San Diego, California." In *Crossing Lines.* 73-96.
Hall, Christine C. Iijima. 1992. "Coloring Outside the Lines." In *Racially Mixed People in America.* 326-329.
Hall, Christine C. Iijima. 1992. "Please Choose One: Ethnic Identity Choices for Biracial Individuals." In *Racially Mixed People in America.* 250-264.
Hall, Christine C. Iijima and Trude I. Cooke Turner. 2001."The Diversity of Biracial Individuals: Asian-White and Asian Minority Biracial Identity." In *The Sum of Our Parts.* 81-92.
Hall, Stuart. 1996. "Gramsci's Relevance for the Study of Race and Ethnicity." In *Stuart Hall: Critical Dialogues in Cultural Studies.* 411-440.
Hall, Stuart. 1997. *Representation: Cultural Representations and Signifying Practices.* London: Sage Publications.
Harris, David R. and Jeremiah Joseph Sim. 2002. "Who Is Multiracial? Assessing the Complexity of Lived Race." *American Sociological Review* Vol. 67, No. 4: 614-627.
Hernandez-Chung, Lilia. 1975. "Race Relations in 'Peninsular' Prose Fiction of the Philippines." *Hispanic Review* Vol. 43, No. 2: 155-167.
Hickman, Christine B. 2003. "The Devil and the 'One Drop' Rule." In *Mixed Race America and Law.* 104-110.
Hirschman, Charles. 1983. "America's Melting Pot Reconsidered." *Annual Review of Sociology* 9: 397-423.
Hollinger, David A. 1995. *Postethnic America.* New York: Basic Books.
Hooks, Bell. 1991. "Essentialism and Experience." *American Literary History* Vol. 3, No. 1: 172-183.

Hooks, Bell. 1981. *Ain't I a Woman: Black Women and Feminism.* Boston: South End Press.
Hooks, Bell. 1984. *Feminist Theory: From Margin to Center.* Cambridge: South End Press.
Hunt, Darnell M. 1999. *O.J. Simpson Facts & Fictions.* Cambridge: Cambridge University Press.
Hwang, Sean-Shong et al. 1997. "Structural and Assimilationist Explanations of Asian-American Intermarriage." *Journal of Marriage and Family* Vol. 59, No. 3: 758-772.
Jacobs, James H. 1992. "Identity Development in Biracial Children." In *Racially Mixed People in America.* 190-206.
Jacobs, Jerry A. and Theresa G. Labov. 2002. "Gender Differentials in Intermarriage among Sixteen Race and Ethnic Groups." *Sociological Forum* Vol. 17, No. 4: 621-646.
Johnson, Kevin R. 2003. *Mixed Race American and the Law.* New York: New York University Press.
Katz, Bruce. 2006. "Concentrated Poverty in New Orleans and Other American Cities." *The Chronicle of Higher Education* Vol. 52, Iss. 48: B.15.
Kennedy, Randall. 2000. "The Enforcement of Anti-Miscegenation Laws." In *Interracialism.* 140-161.
Kennedy, Randall. 2003. *Interracial Intimacies: Sex, Marriage, Identity, and Adoption.* New York: Pantheon Books.
Kich, George Kitahara. 1995. "In the Margins of Sex and Race: Difference, Marginality, and Flexibility." In *The Multiracial Experience.* 263-276.
Kich, George Kitahara. 1992. "The Developmental Process of Asserting a Biracial, Bicultural Identity." In *Racially Mixed People in America.* 304-320.
King, Rebecca Chiyoko. 2001. "Mirror, Mirror, on the Wall: Mapping Discussions of Feminism, Race, and Beauty in Japanese American Beauty Pageants." In *Sum of Our Parts.* 63-172.
King, Rebecca Chiyoko. 1997. "Multiraciality Reigns Supreme?: Mixed-Race Japanese Americans and the Cherry Blossom Queen Pageant." *Amerasian Journal* 23: 13-128.
King, Rebecca Chiyoko and Kimberly McClain DaCosta. 1995. "Changing Face, Changing Race: The Remaking of Race in the Japanese American and African American Communities." In *The Multiracial Experience.* 227-244.
Kowner, Rotem. 2000. "'Lighter Than Yellow, but Not Enough': Western Discourse on the Japanese 'Race,' 1854-1904." *The Historical Journal* Vol. 43, No. 1: 103-131.
Kozol, Jonathan. 2010. "Savage Inequalities: Children in America's Schools." In *The Social Construction of Different and Inequality.* 290-296.
Kuo, Chia-Ling. 1970. "The Chinese on Long Island—a Pilot Study." *Phylon* Vol. 31, No. 3: 280-289.
Landale, Nancy S. and R.S. Oropesa. 2002. "White, Black, or Puerto Rican? Racial Self-Identity Station among Mainland and Island Puerto Ricans." *Social Forces* Vol. 81, No. 1: 231-254.
Lao, Oscar et al. 2006. "Proportioning Whole Genome Single Nucleotide Polymorphism Diversity for the Identification of Geographic Population

Structure and Genetic Ancestry." *American Journal of Human Genetics* Vol. 78, Iss. 4: 680.

Larkin, John A. 1982. "Philippine History Reconsidered: a Social Economic Perspective." *The American Historical Review* Vol. 87, No. 3: 595-628.

Le, C. N. 2006. "Interracial Dating and Marriage." Asian Nation: the Landscape of Asian America. http://www.asian-nation.org/interracials.html.

LaViolette, Forrest and K. H. Silvert. 1951. "The Theory of Stereotypes." *Social Forces* Vol. 29, No. 3: 257-262.

Levy, Yagil. 1998. "Militarizing Inequality: A Conceptual Framework." *Theory and Society* Vol. 27, No. 6: 873-904.

Lewis, Herbert S. 1998. "Anthropology and Race, Then and Now: Commentary on K. Visweswaran, 'Race and Culture of Anthropology.'" *American Anthropologist*, New Series, Vol. 100, No. 4: 979-981.

Liang, Zai and Naomi Ito. 1999. "Intermarriage of Asian Americans in the New York City Region: Contemporary Patterns and Future Prospects." *International Migration Review* Vol. 33, No. 4: 876-900.

Lindsey, Linda L. and Stephen Beach. 2003. *Him she*. Upper Saddle River: Prentice-Hall.

Lipsitz, George. 1998. *The Possessive Investment in Whiteness*. Philadelphia: Temple University Press.

Lopez, Ian F. Haney. 1996. *White By Law*. New York: New York University Press.

Lopez, Ian F. Haney. 2003. "The Social Construction of Race: Some Observations on Illusion, Fabrication, And Choice." In *Mixed Race America and the Law*. 101-103.

Lorber, Judith. 2010. "The Social Construction of Gender." In *The Social Construction of Difference and Inequality*. 112-119.

Loveman, Mara. 1999. "Is 'Race' Essential?" *American Sociological Review* Vol. 64, No. 6: 891-898.

Mahtani, Minelle and April Moreno. 2002. "Same Difference: Towards a More Unified Discourse in 'Mixed Race' Theory." In *Rethinking 'Mixed Race.'* 65-75.

Marable, Manning. 1995. *Beyond Black & White*. London: Verso.

Marx, Anthony W. 1998. *Making Race and Nation: A Comparison of the United States, South Africa, and Brazil*. Cambridge: Cambridge University Press.

Mass, Amy Iwasaki. 1992. "Interracial Japanese Americans: The Best of Both Worlds or the End of the Japanese American Community?" In *Racially Mixed People in America*. 265-279.

McGovney, Dudley O. 2003. "Naturalization of the Mixed-Blood: A Dictum." In *Mixed Race America and the Law*. 407-410.

Mengel, Laurie M. 2002. "Triples—The Social Evolution of a Multiracial Panethnicity." In *Rethinking 'Mixed Race.'* 99-116.

Merton, Robert K. 1995. "The Thomas Theorem and the Matthew Effect." *Social Forces* Vol. 74, No. 2: 379-422.

Messner, M. A. 1997. *Politics of Masculinity: Men in Movements*. Thousand Oaks: Sage Publications.

Messner, M. A. 1992. *Power at Play: Sports and the Problem of Masculinity*. Boston: Beacon.

Mezey, Naomi. 2003. "Erasure and Recognition: The Census, Race and the National Imagination." *Northwestern University Law Review* Vol. 97, Iss. 4: 1701.
Michaels, Walter Benn. 1994. "The No-Drop Rule." *Critical Inquiry* Vol. 20, No. 4, Symposium on "God." 758-769.
Miller, Robin L. 1992. "The Human Ecology of Multiracial Identity." In *Racially Mixed People in America*. 24-36.
Morris-Suzuki, Tessa. 1998. "The Debating Racial Science in Wartime Japan." *Osiris*, 2nd Series, Vol. 13, Beyond Joseph Needham: Science, Technology, and Medicine in East and Southeast Asia. 354-375.
Moskos, Charles C. 1976. "The Military." *Annual Review of Sociology* 2: 55-77.
Motoyoshi, Michelle M. 1990. "The Experience of Mixed-Race People: Some Thoughts and Theories." In the *Journal of Ethnic Studies* 18: 2, 77-94.
Root, Maria P.P. 1996. *The Multiracial Experience*. Thousand Oaks, Sage Publications.
Nakashima, Cynthia L. 1992. "An Invisible Monster: The Creation and Denial of Mixed-Race People in America." In *Racially Mixed People in America*. 162-178.
Nakashima, Cynthia L. 2001. "A Rose by Any Other Name: Names, Multiracial/Multiethnic People, and the Politics of Identity." In *Sum of Our Parts*. 111-120.
Nakashima, Cynthia L. 1995. "Voices From the Movement: Approaches to Multiraciality." In *The Multiracial Experience*. 79-100.
Nash, Philip. 1992. "Multiracial Identity and the Death of Stereotypes." In *Racially Mixed People in America*. 330-332.
Nash, Philip Tajitsu. 1997. "Will the Census Go Multiracial?" In the *Amerasian Journal* 23: 1, 17-27.
National Conference of Christians and Jews. http://mb-soft.com/believe/txn/chrisjew.htm.
National Conference for Community and Justice. http://www.nccj.org.
Ngozi-Brown, Scot. 1997. "African American Soldiers and Filipinos: Racial Imperialism, Jim Crow and Social Relations." *The Journal of Negro History* Vol. 82, No. 1: 42-53.
Ogawa, Dennis Masaaki. 1971. "Small-Group Communication Stereotypes of Black Americans." *Journal of Black Studies* Vol. 1, No. 3: 273-281.
Ogburn, William Fielding. 1937. "Culture and Sociology." *Social Forces* Vol. 16, No. 2: 161-169.
Oliver, Melvin L. and Thomas M. Shapiro. 1995. *Black Wealth/White Wealth: A New Perspective on Racial Inequality*. New York: Routledge.
Omi, Michael. 2001. "Introduction to *Sum of Our Parts*." In *Sum of Our Parts*, ix-xiv.
Omi, Michael and Dana Y. Takagi. 1996. "Situating Asian-Americans in the Political Discourse on Affirmative Action." *Representations* 55, Special Issue: Race and Representation: Affirmative Action. 155-162.
Omi, Michael and Howard Winant. 1994. *Racial Formation in the Untied States*. New York: Routledge.
Ore, Tracy E. 2006. *The Social Construction of Difference in Inequality: Race, Class, Gender, Sexuality*. Third Edition. Boston: McGraw-Hill.
Park, Robert E. 1950. *Race and Culture*. Glencoe: Free Press.

Patterson, Orlando. 1997. *The Ordeal of Integration.* Washington D.C.: Counterpoint.

Penha-Lopes, Vania. 1996. "What Next? On Race and Assimilation in the United States and Brazil." *Journal of Black Studies* Vol. 26, Iss. 6: 809-826.

PR Newswire. 2006. "State of Sickle Cell Disease Is Focus of National Meeting Taking Place in Dallas; Forum Timed for a National Sickle Cell Disease Awareness Month; Is Largest Conference on Disease and Its Ramifications." September 21.

Ramirez, Deborah A. 1995. "Multiracial Identity in a Color-Conscious World." In *The Multiracial Experience.* 49-62.

Root, Maria P.P. 1992. *Racially Mixed People in America.* Newbury Park: Sage Publications.

Reimers, David M. 1992. *Still the Golden Door.* New York: Columbia University Press.

Parker, David and Miri Song. 2001. *Rethinking 'Mixed Race.'* London: Pluto Press.

Rieder, Jonathan. 1985. *Canarsie: The Jews and Italians of Brooklyn against Liberalism.* Cambridge: Harvard University Press.

Rockquemore, Kerry Ann et al. 2009. "Racing to Theory or Retheorizing Race? Understanding the Struggle to Build a Multiracial Identity Theory." *Journal of Social Issues* Vol. 65, No. 1: 13-34.

Roediger, David R. 1991. *The Wages of Whiteness: Race and the Making of the American Working Class.* London: Verso.

Root, Maria P.P. 1992. "Back to the Drawing Board: Methodological Issues in Research on Multiracial People." In *Racially Mixed People in America.* 181-189.

Root, Maria P.P. 2001. "Factors Influencing the Variation in Racial and Ethnic Identity of Mixed-Heritage Persons of Asian Ancestry." In *The Sum of Our Parts.* 61-70.

Root, Maria P. P. 1992. "From Short Cuts to Solutions." In *Racially Mixed People in America.* 342-347.

Root, Maria P.P. 1997. "Multiracial Asians: Models of Ethnic Identity." In the *Amerasian Journal* 23: 29-41.

Root, Maria P.P. 1992. "Within, Between, and Beyond Race." In *Racially Mixed People in America.* 3-11.

Ropp, Steven Masami. 1997. "Do Multiracial Subjects Really Challenge Race? Mixed-Race Asians in the United States and the Caribbean." In the *Amerasian Journal* 23: 1-15.

Saenz, Rogelio et al. 1994. "In Search of Asian War Brides." *Demography* Vol. 31, No. 3: 549-559.

Saito, Leland T. 1998. *Race and Politics: Asian Americans, Latinos, and Whites in a Los Angeles Suburb.* Chicago: University Of Illinois Press.

Schneider, Linda and Arnold Silverman. 2003. *Global Sociology: Introducing Five Contemporary Societies.* Third Edition. Boston: McGraw-Hill.

Sellers, Robert M. et al. 2003. "Racial Identity, Racial Discrimination, Perceived Stress, and Psychological Distress among African-American Young Adults." *Journal of Health and Social Behavior* Vol. 44, No. 3, Special Issue: Race, Ethnicity, and Mental Health. 302-317.

Small, Stephen. 2002. "Colour, Culture and Class; Interrogating Interracial Marriage and People of Mixed Racial Decent in the USA." In *Rethinking 'Mixed Race.'* 117-133.
Smiley, Charles W. 1977. "The Flower Children of Sudbury." *The Family Coordinator* Vol. 26, No. 1: 65-68.
Smythe, H. H. 1953. "Note on the Racial Ideas of the Japanese." *Social Forces* Vol. 31, No. 3: 258-260.
Smythe, Hugh and Yoshimasa Naito. 1953. "The Eta Caste in Japan." *Phylon* Vol. 14, No. 1: 19-27.
Snipp, C. Matthew. 2003. "Racial Measurement and the American Census: Past Practices and Implications for the Future." *Annual Review of Sociology* 29: 563.
Sollors, Werner. 2000. *Interracialism*. Oxford: Oxford University Press.
Spates, James L. 1976. "Counterculture and Dominant Culture Values: A Cross-National Analysis Of the Underground Press and Dominate Culture Magazines." *American Sociological Review* Vol. 41, No. 5: 868-883.
Spencer, Jon Michael. 1997. *The New Colored People*. New York: New York University Press.
Spencer, Rainier. 1999. *Spurious Issues*. Boulder: Westview Press.
Spikard, Paul R. 1992. "The Illogic of American Racial Categories." In *Racially Mixed People in America*. 12-23.
Standen, Brian Chol Soo. 1995. "Without a Template: The Biracial Korean/White Experience." In *The Multiracial Experience*. 245-262.
Steinberg, Stephen. 1995. *Turning Back*. Boston: Beacon Press.
Stephan, Cookie White. 1992. "Mixed-Heritage Individuals: Ethnic Identity and Trait Characteristics." In *Racially Mixed People in America*. 50-63.
Streeter, Caroline A. 1995. "Ambiguous Bodies: Locating Black/White Women in Cultural Representations. In *The Multiracial Experience*. 305-322.
Morley, David and Kuan-Hsing Chen. 1996. *Stuart Hall*. New York: Routledge.
Williams-Leon, Teresa and Cynthia L. Nakashima. 2001. *The Sum of Our Parts*. Philadelphia: Temple University Press.
Takaki, Ronald. 1989. *Strangers from a Different Shore*. Boston: Little, Brown and Company.
Thomas, W.I. and Dorothy Swayne Thomas. 1928. *The Child in America: Behavior Problems and Programs*. City? Knopf.
Thornton, Michael C. 2001. "Black, Japanese, and American: An Asian American Identity Yesterday and Today." In *The Sum of Our Parts*. 93-106.
Thornton, Michael C. 1995. "Hidden Agendas, Identity Theories, and Multiracial People." In *The Multiracial Experience*. 101-120.
Thornton, Michael C. 1992. "Is Multiracial Status Unique? The Personal and Social Experience." In *Racially Mixed People in America*. 321-325.
Thornton, Michael C. 1992. "The Quiet Immigration: Foreign Spouses of U.S. Citizens, 1945-1985." In *Racially Mixed People in America*. 64-76.
Twine, Frances Winddance. 1995. "Heterosexual Alliances: The Romantic Management of Racial Identity." In *The Multiracial Experience*. 291-304.
Tyner, James A. 1999. "The Geopolitics of Eugenics and the Exclusion of Philippine Immigrants from the United States." *Geographical Review* Vol. 89, No. 1: 54-73.

U.S. Census Bureau. "People Quick Facts." http://quickfacts.census.gov/qfd/states/00000.html.

Valverde, Kieu-Linh Caroline. 2001. "Doing the Mixed-Race Dance: Negotiating Social Spaces Within the Multiracial Vietnamese American Class Typology." In *Sum of Our Parts*. 131-144.

Vritanen Simo V. and Leonie Huddy. 1998. "Old-Fashioned Racism and New Forms of Racial Prejudice." *The Journal of Politics* Vol. 60, No. 2: 311-332.

Waddlington, Walter. 2003. "The Loving Case: Virginia's Anti-Miscegenation Statute In Historical Perspective." In *Mixed Race America and the Law*. 53-55.

Waters, Mary C. 1990. *Ethnic Options*. Berkeley: University of California Press.

Weightman, George H. 1967. "The Philippine—Chinese Image of the Filipino." *Pacific Affairs* Vol. 40, No. 3/4: 315-323.

Weisman, Jan R. 2001. "The Tiger and His Stripes: Thai and American Reactions to Tiger Wood's (Multi) 'Racial Self.'" In *The Sum of Our Parts*. 231-244.

Weitz, Rose. 2001. "Women and Their Hair: Seeking Power through Resistance and Accommodation." *Gender and Society* Vol. 15, No. 5: 667-686.

White, Shane and Graham White. 1995. "Slave Hair and African-American Culture and 18th and 19th Centuries." *The Journal of Southern History* Vol. 61, No. 1: 45-76.

Williams, Teresa Kay. 1992. "Prism Lives: Identity of Binational Amerasians." In *Racially Mixed People in America*. 280-303.

Williams, Teresa Kay. 1995. "Race as Process: Reassessing the 'What Are You?' Encounters of Biracial Individuals." In *The Multiracial Experience*. 191-210.

Williams-Leon, Teresa. 2001. "The Convergence of Passing Zones: Multiracial Gays, Lesbians, and Bisexuals of Asian Descent." In *The Sum of Our Parts*. 145-162.

Wilson, William Julius. 1978. *The Declining Significance of Race: Blacks and Changing American Institutions*. Chicago: The University Of Chicago Press.

Wilson, William Julius. 1996. *When Work Disappears: The World of the New Urban Poor*. New York: Vintage Books.

Winant, Howard. 2000. "Race and Race Theory." *This* 26: 169-185.

Winant, Howard. 2001. *The World is a Ghetto*. New York: Basic Books.

Xie, Yu and Kimberly Goyette. 1997. "The Racial Identification of Biracial Children with One Asian Parent: Evidence from the 1990 Census." *Social Forces* Vol. 76, No. 2: 547-570.

Yancey, George. 2003. *Who is White? Latinos, Asians, and the New Black/Nonblack Divide*. Boulder: Lynne Rienner Publishers.

Zack, Naomi. 1995. *American Mixed Race*. Lanham: Rowman & Littlefield Publishers, Inc.

Zack, Naomi. 1993. *Race and Mixed Race*. Philadelphia: Temple University Press.

Index

Accent 66
Ambiguous/Ambiguity 3, 12, 27, 28, 38, 67, 90, 96, 121, 143
African 13,
American Ethnicity/Identity 17, 25
American Friends Service Group 109
Americanization 26
Ancestry 8
Anglo Conformity 17, 26, 38, 47, 54, 138
Anti-miscegenation laws 9, 13, 59, 107, 111
Anytown 110
Asian Indians 14
Assimilation 2, 15, 16, 18, 19, 25, 26, 30, 35, 53, 54, 76, 102, 105, 106, 107, 121, 126, 129, 135, 137, 138, 139, 140
   Attitudinal 81
   Behavior Receptional 80, 81
Association of Multi-Ethnic Americans (AMEA) 14, 15
Barbarian 114
Black Couples 3
Blackness 3, 18
Black/white 12, 13
Bridges 3
Brubaker, Roger 23
Caucasian 14
Chinese 6, 9, 12
Christian 108, 110, 116, 119
Civil Rights 10
Class/Classes 7, 8
Color 12, 113, 115, 117, 118
Concept of Race 2, 7, 8, 11, 15, 20, 71
Constrained 80, 84, 85, 89, 92, 139, 140
Constructivist 23, 24
Cooper, Fredrick 23
Creoles 12
Cultural attributes 68, 69, 77, 95, 111
Cultural Identity 23, 24, 35
Davis, F. James 37

Discrimination/Discriminate 3, 10, 11, 29, 120
Diverse racial background/heritage 6, 7, 21
Espiritu, Yen 46, 81, 110
Essential/Essentialist 2, 10, 19, 20, 23, 24, 30, 32, 34, 45, 55, 68, 113, 139
Eta 9, 10
Ethnic Identification/identity 4, 25
Ethnicity 2, 15, 16, 17, 18, 105
Ethno-racial pentagon 79
European ethnicities 2
Exotic 96, 97
Food 74
French 12
Gaskins, Pearl 24, 28
Gender 6, 7
Gordon, Milton 16
Harris, David 26
Heritage 8, 10, 30
Hierarchy 8, 26, 87, 100, 105, 106, 107, 113, 114, 137, 140
Hindu 9
Hispanic 39, 45, 63, 65, 66, 67
Hollinger, David 15, 37, 79
Hyper-descent 17, 18
Hypo-descent 17, 18, 55
Identity 3, 4, 20
Ideology/Ideologies 3, 4, 9, 10, 113, 141
Inequality 10
Indians 12
Intermarry/Intermarriage 2, 4, 10, 18, 105, 106, 107, 116, 117, 121, 126, 135
Interracial
   Dating 116, 129
   Families 3, 59, 140
   Marriage(s) 3, 4, 16, 105, 110, 115, 123, 129, 137, 139, 140
   Parents 5
   Relationships 58, 107
Interviewees

Index

Ai 59, 60, 64, 65, 66, 69, 86, 95
Aiko 36, 37, 51, 52, 67, 87, 88, 91, 98, 99
Alexandria 108, 115, 116, 117, 118, 119
Ben 125
Brad 46
Cornelius 39, 40, 64, 65, 73, 89
David 39, 41, 42
Elizabeth 96, 98, 99
Francine 39, 40, 75
Gerald 45, 72
James 32, 38, 46, 63, 65, 70, 72, 74, 75, 131, 132
James (parent) 124
Jane 31, 47, 51, 88, 96, 99, 136, 137
Jasmine 124
John 29, 32, 41, 42, 43, 44, 51
Josh 31, 39, 41, 42, 44, 46, 47, 48, 49, 75, 81
Karen 41, 42, 43, 134, 135
Lamont 36, 37, 39, 64, 65, 87, 91
Lenny 32, 39, 40, 45, 47, 129, 130
Leonard 40, 41, 44, 45, 49, 50, 130, 131
Mandy 31, 33, 35, 69, 71, 72
Margaret 27, 28, 37, 38, 54, 67, 90
Masako 122, 123, 128
Melvin 110, 111, 118
Misa 124, 126, 128
Miyoko 122, 123, 126
Ron 33, 35
Rosie 109, 112, 113, 115, 120
Rudy 39, 40, 65, 82, 83
Sabrina 28, 67, 81, 89
Sumi 33, 73, 94
Ted 109, 111, 113, 114, 115, 120
Theo 30, 32, 33, 75, 76, 90, 95
Timothy 41, 42, 43, 44, 100
Tomoko 41
Tyrone 36, 37, 44, 62, 63, 66, 74, 86, 90, 92, 95, 101
Japanese 1, 2, 9, 14, 17, 18, 66
Jim Crow laws 9, 13
King, Rebecca 96
Kinship 8
Korean 9
Kurombo 86
Landale 63
Latino 38, 42, 50
Lipsitz, George 11
Lopez, Ian 13, 19, 134
Macro level 2, 14, 20
Mainstream culture 2
Melting Pot 26, 37, 38, 47, 123, 140
Mestizos 62
Mexican 13, 39, 40, 45, 65
Michaels, Walter 23, 24
Micro level 2, 14, 20
Military 6
Minority/minority 4
Mixed-race 4
Mono-racial 3, 30, 143, 144
Mulatto(s) 12, 13
Multiracial
　Activists 4
　Category 15
　Children 14, 15, 16, 20
　Construct 15
　Discourse 16, 18
　Experience 15
　Heritage 3, 15, 26, 28
　Identity 15, 28, 30, 55
　Project 18, 25, 29, 30, 55, 80, 107, 139, 140, 141
　Society 2
Nationality 1, 13, 27, 28
Native Americans 12, 13, 17, 18
Nigger 86, 90, 103, 118
Octoroon 12
Office of Management and Budget (OMB) 14
Omi, Michael 18, 19, 93
One drop rule 13, 17, 30, 54, 116, 133, 140
Oriental 123, 124, 125
Ozawa v. United States 13
Pacific Islander 31, 41, 64
Pan-ethnicity 21, 45, 46, 81
Park, Robert 15, 16
Passing 12, 54, 95
People of color 15
Phenotype 10
Physical characteristics 8
Possessive investment in whiteness 11
Push/pull factors 69, 103

Primordial 110
Project RACE 14, 15
Quadroon 12
Race relations cycle 15
Race/Racial
    Classification 13, 18
    Characteristics 12, 31, 32
    Common sense 1, 13, 14, 19, 27
    Constructs 10
    Experiences 4
    Formations 18, 19, 25, 26, 80
    Groups 4
    Hegemony 80
    Hierarchy 1, 2, 11, 12, 21, 27, 45, 53, 55, 68, 77, 86
    Justice 2
    Logic 1, 14, 19, 20, 26, 27, 55, 57, 65, 72, 73
    Mixture 5
    Project 2, 9, 18, 19
    Purity 57, 58
    Socially constructed 2
    Stratification 11
Racial Identity 2, 23, 24, 26, 43, 44
    Constrained 24
    Expressed 20, 26, 28, 48, 49, 50, 68, 74, 76, 82
    External 20, 26, 27, 34, 36, 38, 59, 61, 63, 66, 68, 76, 93, 94
    Internal 20, 26, 29, 30, 34, 35, 36, 37, 45, 47, 55, 60, 61, 62, 63, 66, 68, 69, 70, 74, 75, 76, 82, 84, 89, 99
Racialized 24, 121, 123
Racism 3, 4, 12, 21, 58, 81, 86, 87, 88, 89, 92, 93, 107, 116, 123, 140
Racist 3, 115, 119, 139, 140
Rational 80, 84, 89, 92, 126, 140
Reify/Reified 3, 13
Sample/Sampling 5
    Snowball 5, 143
    Representative 6
Samoan 42, 43
San Diego 6,
Self Identification 14
Sim, Jeremiah 26
Socio-historical 8, 12, 18, 19
Social Status 12
Socially Constructed/Social Construction 7, 9, 10, 11, 12, 13, 20, 28, 29, 32, 53, 55, 73, 79, 116, 141
Spanish 12, 13
Sports 100
Stereotypes 9, 68, 69, 70, 71, 72, 73, 77, 124
Strategic race 47, 48, 53, 55
Susan Guillory Phipps 23
Symbolic ethnicity 25, 35, 47
Symbolic race 47
Thomas Theorem 20
US
    Census 4, 12, 14, 17, 143
    Constitution 11, 12,
    Supreme Court 13,
    v. Thind 14,
Waters, Mary 25, 26, 35, 47
Westside Story 110
"What are you?" 20, 24, 26, 27, 28, 53, 55
White/black 2, 17, 24, 89, 122, 134, 138, 139
White/minority 4,
White privilege 62, 82, 117, 118, 119, 128, 130, 131, 133, 137, 140
White supremacy 5, 102, 117, 132, 136, 141
Winant, Howard 18, 19, 93, 117
Woods, Tiger 3, 29
World War II 58, 59, 86, 117

About the Book

What does it mean for an Asian American to be part white—or part black? Bruce Hoskins probes the experience of biracial Asian Americans, revealing the ways that our discourse about multiracial identities too often reinforces racial hierarchies.

Hoskins explores the everyday lives of people of Asian/white and Asian/black heritage to uncover the role of our society's white-black continuum in shaping racial identity. Mixing intimate personal stories with cutting-edge theoretical analysis, he directly confronts the notion that multiracial identity provides an easy solution for our society's racial stratification.

Bruce Calvin Hoskins is professor of sociology at MiraCosta College.